The Post-war Restitution of Property Rights in Europe

The Post-war Restitution of Property Rights in Europe

Comparative Perspectives

Wouter Veraart & Laurens Winkel (eds.)

with contributions by

Claire Andrieu
Georg Graf
Jürgen Lillteicher
Franz-Stefan Meissel
Herman C.F. Schoordijk
Arend Soeteman
Veerle Vanden Daelen
Wouter Veraart
Laurens Winkel

RVP PRESS
New York 2012

RVP Publishers Inc.
95 Morton Street, Ground Floor
New York, NY 10014

RVP Press, New York

cover image: Alma Mahler Werfel

© 2012 Kloof Booksellers, Amsterdam & Scientia Verlag, Aalen on behalf of the individual authors / RVP Publishers Inc., New York

Edvard Munch: Summer Night on the Beach, 1902-03 (p. 50)
© 2012 The Munch Museum / The Munch-Ellingsen Group / Artists Rights Society (ARS), NY

No part of this book may be translated or reproduced in any form, by print, photoprint, microfilm, or by any other means, without written permission of the publisher.

Papers presented at an international conference held April 26, 2006 in Rotterdam. Includes bibliographical references, name index and subject index.

RVP Press™ is an imprint of RVP Publishers Inc., New York
The RVP Publishers logo is a registered trademark of RVP Publishers Inc., New York

Library of Congress Control Number: 2011934285

ISBN 978 1 61861 339 4

www.rvppress.com

Table of contents

An Introduction to Dilemmas of Post-War Restitution in Europe 1
    Wouter Veraart & Laurens Winkel

Post-war Restitution *versus* Present-day Reparation in France: Towards
the Disappearance of Legal and Political Dilemmas? 11
    Claire Andrieu

Contrasting Legal Concepts of Restitution in France and the Netherlands 21
    Wouter Veraart

The Restitution of 'Aryanized' Property – Recent developments in
Austrian Law... 35
    Georg Graf

The Restitution of the Munch Painting *Summer Night on the Beach*
under the Austrian Art Restitution Act 1998 47
    Franz-Stefan Meissel

Who is a victim of Nazism? West Germany and its approach to private
participation in the Aryanization Policy during the Nazi Era.................... 79
    Jürgen Lillteicher

Consequences of Persecution: Antwerp as an Example of Restitution in
Belgium (1944-1960) in Comparative Perspective with the Netherlands .. 93
    Veerle Vanden Daelen

The Goudstikker Case.. 109
    Herman C.F. Schoordijk

Risks of Open Norms. A Reply to Schoordijk.. 119
    Arend Soeteman

Authors... 123

Name Index 125

Subject Index 129

An Introduction to Dilemmas of Post-War Restitution in Europe

Wouter VERAART[*] & Laurens WINKEL

Despite possibly being of importance for legal historians, prior to 1989 the whole idea of reconsidering post war restitution and the related legal problems was not on the political and legal agenda. After 1989, however, restitution of property rights in the wake of periods of serious injustice has become a global phenomenon. However, in 1995, exactly fifty years after WWII, the disclosure that Swiss banks still held a considerable number of bank accounts of Jewish Nazi victims, never claimed by their heirs, caused a worldwide public outcry.[1] Since then, and especially in the late 1990s, innumerable countries have been dealing with their unjust pasts. Some of them have embarked on complex projects of transitional justice which are far from finished. These include most Eastern European countries dealing with their communist pasts[2], and post-apartheid South Africa, struggling to overcome the heritage of apartheid by a politics of redistribution and reconciliation.[3] In the late 1990s Europe faced a 'revival' of Holocaust-related claims. Some of these claims had never been dealt with before, as in large parts of Eastern Europe. In other cases they had been dealt with in earlier decades, but – as the argument went – in a flawed and formalistic way. In those cases the claimants called for a new round in the restitution of 'Holocaust-assets', this time based on historical fact-finding by independent research commissions, and hopefully a more generous attitude from states, banks, insurance companies, and other parties, public or private, who took benefit from the massive spoliation of the European Jews during the Second World War. Restitution issues, however, were not limited to the European continent and South Africa. In other parts of the world, restitution issues often involved indigenous peoples trying to settle land claims dating from centuries of oppression, exclusion and expropriation.[4]

---

[*] Veraart contributed to this article in the context of his research project 'Time, Restitution and the Law', financed by the Netherlands Organisation for Scientific Research.
[1] See Th. Maissen, *Verweigerte Erinnerung. Nachrichtenlose Vermögen und Schweizer Weltkriegsdebatte 1989-2004* (Zürich 2005).
[2] See I. Pogany, *Righting wrongs in Western Europe* (Manchester/ New York 1997).
[3] See e.g. Wouter Veraart, 'Redressing the Past with an Eye to the Future. The Impact of the Passage of Time on Property Rights Restitution in Post-Apartheid South-Africa', *Netherlands Quarterly of Human Rights* 27/1 (2009), pp. 45-60.
[4] See D. Celermajer, *The Sins of the Nation and the Ritual of Apologies* (Cambridge 2009); J. Thompson, *Taking Responsibility for the Past. Reparation and Historical Injustice* (Cambridge/ Malden 2002).

Dealing with restitution of property rights in a context of transitional justice involves many dilemmas. In this book, some of these dilemmas will be discussed in the context of restitution processes in the aftermath of WWII in France, the Netherlands, Austria, Germany and Belgium, in the years 1945-2005. The scope of this book is strictly limited to the way these European countries have dealt with the atrocities of their Nazi past, as a result of German occupation or otherwise. The deprivation of property rights occurred in the context of the persecution and genocide of the European Jews in the period 1938-1945. Of course, the authors only deal with some aspects of these complex and comprehensive histories.

A focus on these (Western) European countries also makes room for comparisons. One common thread throughout the different articles, written by historical and legal experts in the field, is the impact of the passage of time on restitution issues. Time-related questions are manifold and include problems of legal applicability and legal closure. On the one hand, the principle of non-retroactivity of laws, statutes of limitation and the legal concept of prescription may prevent restitution from taking place. On the other hand, the demand for restitution may become so strong that statutes of limitation may be suspended and past court decisions become subject to review when, according to new insights, they have been insufficiently fair in light of the extreme injustice of the past.[5]

Another time-related aspect is the changing character of restitution policies and processes. In the 1990s, many countries in Europe faced a new round in their respective restitution processes concerning Holocaust-related claims. However, as Claire Andrieu points out in her chapter on France, nature and character of the developments in the 1990s were completely different from the first restitution cycle in the late 1940s and 1950s. Although Andrieu is only considering the French case, her remarks have a broader, European, significance. First, Andrieu points out that the strictly legal approach from the 1940s and 1950s has been replaced in the 1990s by a much more openly moral, policy-oriented approach. Whereas 'equality before the law' had been a leading principle during the 1940s and 1950s, in the 1990s it is much more 'equity' that has been imposing itself as a dominant moral value in matters of restitution, sometimes at the expense of the principle of legal equality. Second, whereas previously restitution laws and policies had a strictly national character, the major developments in Europe in the 1990s were triggered by global media-campaigns and serious economic and political pressure from the United States. Moreover, American *class actions*, initiated on behalf of unspecified groups of victims targeting European banks and insurance companies with strong economic presence in the US, intersected with the 'closed' legal systems of individual European

---

5 See Wouter Veraart, *De passie voor een alledaagse rechtsorde. Over vergeten, herinneren en vergeven als reacties op historisch onrecht* (Den Haag 2010), pp. 9-25.

nations states, leaving the latter's quest for legal closure redundant.[6] Third, instead of corrective justice on the basis of which the *individual* claimant is compensated by the specific organisation or person who is legally accountable for a specific wrong in the past, the usual *modus operandi* in the 1990s has been based on the concept of distributive justice: in most cases, *categories* of victims or their heirs have been financially compensated by public and private funding for more generic wrongs from which they suffered, while the relationship between the specific wrong on the individual level and the amount of compensation paid was (much) more distant. One of the reasons for this de-contextualization (cf. Andrieu) is the difficulty of establishing legal proof in the individual case after sixty years or more after the facts; thus, in the 1990s, the painstaking legal process of truth finding in specific cases has been replaced by a more general fact-finding process by independent commissions of historical and legal experts.

Overview of the contributions

The purpose of this book is threefold. First, the authors take care to describe some of the legal aspects of the restitution processes in the 1940s and 1950s in the aforementioned five European countries. The case studies in this book contribute to a better legal-historical understanding of the histories of post-war restitution in these countries. As such, this book complements some earlier publications in this specialized field of study, with less legal and more historical focus.[7] Second, in two chapters, an explicit comparison is made between post-war restitution policies in different European countries. Third, different authors compare the restitution process in the first decades following 1945 with the restitution policies in the 1990s and the first decade of the current century. In this context, they pay attention to time-related restitution dilemmas, as mentioned in the previous paragraph.

Summarizing the different chapters in their order of appearance: in her chapter on France, Claire Andrieu clarifies the difference in approach after 1945 and after 1989. Whereas the Free French under De Gaulle launched a restitution process based on strict legal principles such as equality of all

---

6   See A. Garapon, *Peut-on réparer l'histoire? Colonisation, esclavage, Shoah* (Paris 2008), pp. 255-262.

7   See C. Goschler & Ph. Ther (eds.), *Raub und Restitution. "Arisierung" und Rückerstattung des jüdischen Eigentums in Europa* (Frankfurt am Main 2003), english edition: M. Dean, C. Goschler & Ph. Ther (eds.), *Robbery and Restitution, The Conflict over Jewish Property in Europe* (New York 2007); C. Goschler & J. Lillteicher, *"Arisierung" und Restitution. Die Rückerstattung jüdischen Eigentums in Deutschland und Österreich nach 1945 und 1989* (Göttingen 2002); V. Pawlowsky & H. Wendelin, *Enteignete Kunst. Raub und Rückgabe - Österreich von 1938 bis heute* (Wien 2006); J. Elster (ed.), *Retribution & Reparation in the Transition to Democracy* (Cambridge 2006); D. Diner & G. Wunberg (eds.), *Restitution and Memory. Material Restoration in Europe* (New York 2007).

before the law, the approach after 1989 was much more loosely defined, to the effect that, according to Andrieu, it brought about the "disappearance of legal and political dilemmas".

In his chapter on France and the Netherlands, Wouter Veraart compares the restitution policies in both countries in the years 1943-1952. He concludes that, while the French were committed to the re-establishment of the republican rule of law and understood the restitution of property rights as a necessary part of this endeavour, Dutch policymakers took a much more economic and pragmatic view towards restitution issues. As a consequence, the French opted for strict legal rules to undo 'forced' transactions by which former owners had been deprived of their property rights; while the Dutch used open-ended legal rules and a special court of restoration, equipped with large discretionary powers, which dealt with each case separately.

Georg Graf gives an overview of some interesting recent developments in Austrian law with respect to property that was taken away under or by the Nazi regime and has not since been returned to its original owners or their heirs. In this chapter, he pays special attention to the legal concept of 'extreme injustice', which has been used in Austria in recent years to revise past legal decisions and out-of-court settlements with regard to Nazi-looted property rights. In this context, he also returns to the Austrian restitution legislation of the late 1940s.

Stefan Meissel's chapter on the Austrian restitution case of the Edvard Munch painting *Summer Night on the Beach*, formerly owned by Alma Mahler-Werfel, combines a detailed reconstruction of the legal-historical aspects of this interesting case with a critical legal assessment of its merits. This complex 'looted art' case covers an extended period of time, ranging from the facts concerning the deprivation of the painting in the late 1930s, the first restitution cycle in the 1940s and 1950s, until its *denouement* in 2006. As such, it is a perfect illustration of the chapter by Graf on the more general aspects of the Austrian restitution legislation in the past and present, including the application of the concept of 'extreme injustice' in the first decade of the 21st century.

In his chapter on Germany, Jürgen Lillteicher deals with an issue that has generally been neglected: historically mapping the changing position of private owners of Nazi-looted property in the post-war years. At first, in the Western occupied zones of Germany between 1945 and 1949, 'current owners' were often forced to return their properties to the original, mostly Jewish, owners or their heirs. However, these private 'restitutors' were well organized and those negatively affected have been struggling for compensation for this 'injustice' done to them for many years. In a number of cases they have been partially indemnified for their 'losses' by the Adenauer government after the establishment of the Federal Republic of Germany in 1949. As a consequence, the financial burden shifted from specific private 'restitutors' to the taxpaying collective as a whole. Discussing the details,

Lillteicher points to the fact that changing ideas over individual vs. collective accountability for Nazi-crimes are related to the shift from a 'corrective' to a 'distributive' response to the extreme injustice of the German past.

The contribution of Veerle Vanden Daelen focuses on how the practical and legal consequences of the war were settled for Jews in Belgium, using Antwerp as an example. To put the Belgian situation into a wider perspective she draws comparisons to the situation in the Netherlands. According to Vanden Daelen, the spoliation during the war and the difficult restitution afterwards were similar in both countries, but led to – at least – two different reactions in Belgium and the Netherlands, primarily due to the degree of integration, assimilation and national citizenship of Jews in the respective countries.

In his contribution on the Dutch Goudstikker-case, Herman Schoordijk discusses a case that has been dealt with by the Dutch Advisory Committee on the Assessment of Restitution Applications for items of Cultural Value and the Second World War (in short the 'Restitution Committee'). Since late 2001, this Committee has been advising the Dutch government on returning works of art that were looted by the Nazis, usually from Jewish owners, currently held by the Dutch State. Each claim submitted to the Committee is examined on an individual basis.

We can see from the background behind the decision to set up this Committee that the Dutch government's intention was originally to tie up as many 'loose ends' as possible by seeking, in a generous way, to put right matters relating to looted art that the Dutch authorities responsible had clearly failed to deal with satisfactorily in the immediate post-war years. It was not primarily seeking, however, to reopen cases where final settlement had already been reached. In other words, cases where there had been a court ruling or legally valid settlement in the post-war period. It was only in the event of a *novum* – that is, genuinely new and relevant facts– that the government considered it permissible for a past court decision or a settlement to be amended or reviewed today.

The Restitution Committee, however, chose to pursue a different path by aligning itself with the views of an earlier committee that had looked at the issue of looted art and interpreted the term *novum* more broadly than the government had done. This committee took a *novum* to mean also "the results of changed (historic) views of justice and the consequences of the policy conducted at the time" and, on a later date, stated that "insights and circumstances which, according to generally accepted views, have evidently changed since the Second World War should be granted the status of new facts."[8]

---

8 See K. Lubina, *Contested Cultural Property. The Return of Nazi Spoliated Art and Human Remains from Public Collections*, diss. Maastricht 2009, pp. 299-318.

If a *novum* is defined in a way that also includes 'changed insights', there will in principle be unlimited opportunities to set aside or ignore post-war settlements or judgements. Significantly, it is precisely this reasoning that prompted the decision taken by the Restitution Committee in the famous *Goudstikker* case. Leaving aside the earlier decision taken by the Court of Appeal of The Hague in December 1999[9] and the out-of-court settlement reached in 1952 with the widow of Goudstikker[10], the Committee advised the Dutch State in December 2005 to reopen the case and to return 202 paintings to the Goudstikker heirs. In early 2006, the government decided, under protest, to follow this advice.[11]

In his article Schoordijk argues that, for different reasons, the Restitution Committee was right in its recommendation to return the paintings to the Goudstikker heirs. One of his arguments is that 'equity' as a corrective element to legal formalism has been established itself as a leading principle in private law in the twentieth century. If that is the case, Schoordijk argues, why should it not also be used to correct post-war legal judgments or settlements in restitution cases, if we consider their outcomes, according to current insights, to be unjust? At this point Schoordijk's analysis of the Dutch Goudstikker case comes close to the Austrian discussion about the difficulties surrounding the criterium of 'extreme injustice' as a means to revise past decisions or settlements.

In his reply to Schoordijk, Arend Soeteman argues against Schoordijk's strong plea for 'equity' as a means to correct past injustices. According to Soeteman, the concept of 'equity' is likely to benefit economically powerful parties, but may hurt those parties who are among the most vulnerable in the restitution process.

---

9   *M. von Saher c.s. v the Netherlands*, Court of Appeals The Hague 16 December 1999.
10 Her motifs for renouncing her claims in 1952 were mainly economical: one of the conditions for restitution was that a received purchase price which had come in the free possession of the selling party, should be returned, in this case to the Dutch State. The ratio behind this rule was the principle of unjust enrichment: nobody should take profit out of the process of restitution, not even the dispossessed.) The main reason that the widow Goudstikker did not want to return the purchase price was that she and her advisors expected that the current market value of the paintings would be lower than the price that Goering had paid for them in the summer of 1940; besides she did not intend to restart the artdealer business of her deceased husband. See Muller & Schretlen, *Betwist Bezit* (Zwolle 2002), pp. 205-209.
11 See the Advisory Committee for Restitution Applications for Items of Cultural Value and the Second World War, *Goudstikker-Report* (RC 1.15) (in Dutch), The Hague 2006 and the Advisory Committee for Restitution Applications for Items of Cultural Value and the Second World War, *Goudstikker-Recommendation* (RC 1.15) (in Dutch), The Hague 2006; letter of the deputy minister of Education, Art and Sciences, Medy van der Laan to the chair of the Dutch Parliament, 6 February 2006, available on <http://www.minocw.nl/documenten/5640.pdf>.

Restitution and the passage of time

At the end of this introduction, we would like to make a few historical remarks on the important topic of restitution and the passage of time. First, one can find an example in biblical law of the provisions in Leviticus 25 concerning the jubilee, every fifty years:

> Lev. 25, 10: And ye shall hallow the fiftieth year, and proclaim liberty throughout all the land unto all the inhabitants thereof: it shall be a jubilee unto you; and ye shall return every man unto his possession, and ye shall return every man unto his family.[12]

From this text follows that the 'legal order' as to ownership of land has to start again every fifty years. However, we do not know even in biblical times of the application of this law[13] but in view of the later development of theories of distributive justice, the example remains interesting. A general, not very sophisticated theory behind prescription holds that on the long run the facts and the law have to be in accordance with each other.[14] Rules of prescription can lead therefore to social peace.

Nevertheless, in the most developed legal system in history, Roman law in Antiquity, there was by far no such thing as a consistent theory concerning prescription.[15] On the one hand acquisitive prescription of stolen things was never possible[16], whereas in other cases there was a rather short term for acquisitive prescription in the form of *usucapio*, in classical Roman law either one year for certain movables or two years for certain

---

12 King James Translation.
13 In B.S. Jackson (ed.), *Jewish Law and Legal History and the Modern World* (Leyden 1980), there is, as far as we can see, no reference to this institution. Nevertheless, the first essay by R. Yaron in this book gives an excellent introduction to questions of the relations between the ancient Near Eastern Laws amongst each other. See also M. Hudson, 'Reconstructing the Origins of Interest-Bearing Debt and the Logic of Clean Slates', in: M. Hudson & M. van de Mieroop (eds.), *Debt and Economic Renewal in the Ancient Near East* (Bethesda, Maryland 2002), pp. 7-53, esp. p. 37 ff; R. Westbrook, 'Social Justice in the Ancient Near East', in: *Social Justice in the Ancient World* 1995, pp. 149-163, esp. p. 160 ff; M. Weinfeld, *Social Justice in the Ancient Israel and in the Ancient Near East* (Jerusalem 1995), pp. 152-179; J.S. Bergsma, *The Jubilee from Leviticus to Qumran. A History of Interpretation* (Leyden 2007), pp. 295ff, esp. pp. 297-298. According to Weinfeld is "the institution […] of the Jubilee in Israel […] inherent to tribal society of the pre-monarchical period" (p. 177). We thank our colleague Westbrook who so untimely passed away in January 2009 for his kind help.
14 R. Caterina, *Impium praesidium, le ragioni a favore e contro l'usucapione* (Milano 2001), p. 12 ff.
15 D. Nörr, *Die Entstehung der 'longi temporis praescriptio' – Studien zum Einfluß der Zeit im Recht und zur Rechtspolitik in der Kaiserzeit*, (Köln-Opladen 1966), p. 108 ff.
16 Following from the Law of the XII Tables (450 BC) and the so called *Lex Atinia* (2nd century BC), see M. Kaser, *Das römische Privatrecht*, I, 2nd edition (München 1971), p. 419 ff.

immovables. In later Roman law constitutions of Justinian of 529-531 AD, found in the titles 7,33 to 7,39 of the Codex of Justinian introduced the prescription of actions in a rather confused set of rules with terms going from 10 to 40 years (*praescriptio longi* or *longissimi temporis*). We suppose the length of these terms could have some relation with the average life expectations at that time (± 534 AD) and with the measure of disruption of the legal order that has taken place. In all legal systems of civil law we meet with these terms of 10, 20, 30 or 40 years as a result of the reception of Roman law.[17]

At present, there is a general tendency against prescription in both criminal law and private law. According to the Dutch Criminal Code, the prescription of prosecution does not exist anymore for all crimes for which life imprisonment is provided (art. 70), a provision which was introduced only quite recently. In international criminal law there is, since 1968, no prescription for crimes against humanity and war crimes. It is not clear whether this tendency remains under the spell of common law influence, where there has traditionally never been prescription in favour of e.g. the thief[18]. In private law there is nearly worldwide hesitation concerning prescription in cases of transitional justice – the situation after the change of regime and more specifically, in the case of restitution claims after the Second World War.

Some elements of legal theory behind prescription may be advanced, albeit not very elaborate. At first, one could think of the aforementioned distinction Aristotle already made between distributive and corrective justice in the Nicomachean Ethics, book V. Here Aristotle distinguishes between an original situation as a result of distributive justice and the redress, result of corrective justice, after a disruption of the original situation created by distributive justice.[19] When the mechanism of corrective justice fails to set in, prescription would finally lead to an acceptance of the disruption of the original situation. Apparently, Aristotle does not mention prescription as part of his theory of justice. An explanation for this could be that prescription only occasionally occurred in the Greek legal reality.[20] In modern legal theory the theory of justice of Aristotle still plays an important role, which can be seen in the works of E.J. Weinrib[21] and William Lucy.[22] In modern

---

17 Cf. Dutch Civil Code art. 3: 99-106 and 3: 306.
18 W.J. Zwalve, *C. Æ. Uniken Venema's Common Law & Civil Law* (Deventer 2000), p. 106 ff, quotes the English Limitation Act of 1980 and expounds that common law does not know acquisitive prescription, but only extinctive prescription, but never in the case of theft.
19 See I. Englard, *Corrective and Distributive Justice. From Aristotle to Modern Times* (Oxford 2009), pp. 1-10; 177 ff.
20 A short survey in J. H. Lipsius, *Attisches Recht und Rechtsverfahren* (repr. Aalen 1966), p. 676 note 5; see also J.W. Jones, *The Law and Legal Theory of the Greeks* (Oxford 1956, repr. Aalen 1977), pp. 233; 302.
21 E.J. Weinrib, *The Idea of Private Law* (Cambridge Mass. 1995), pp. 56 ff.

legal thought one could also think of Rawls's concept of the original position as a – since Kant – nearly always hypothetical, but important point of orientation.[23]

Prescription as a legal institution has evidently a link with the development of the concept and theory of private property[24] and the law of succession.[25] Not without good reason is the annulment of a settlement difficult and practically always excluded. This goes back to ancient principles about settlement. In Roman law there are several texts prohibiting the annulment of a *transactio*[26] in cases of mistake. A distinction is made between mistakes of fact or of law.[27] In the latter case annulment is prohibited, in the former case there are a few possibilities of overthrowing a transaction. In the articles of Graf, Meissel and Schoordijk, discussing Austrian and Dutch 'looted art' cases, this argument plays an important role.

The concept of prescription is more broadly linked with the authority of decided cases[28], a principle which is not unrestrictedly applicable in private law disputes, but nevertheless gives a certain guideline. What has been said about judicial decisions can be enlarged to arbitration law. According to international rules concerning arbitration it is only possible in very exceptional circumstances to contest the result of the arbitrators' decision. For Dutch law this follows from art. 1064 of the Code of Civil Procedure.

In modern legal theory some attention has been paid to the relation between the concept of justice and the elapse of time. The French legal philosopher Pierre Hébraud deals with the notion of prescription, roughly within the theoretical framework of temporality in the 'Théorie des Institu-

---

22 W. Lucy, *Philosophy of Private Law* (Oxford 2007), pp. 268–375.
23 J. Rawls, *A Theory of Justice*, (Cambridge Mass. 1971), p. 12 ff. some German legal philosophers reproach Rawls to set back legal philosophy to the 18th century, see e.g. J. Habermas, *Faktizität und Geltung*, 4th edition (Darmstadt 1994), p. 79, quoted by Theo Mayer-Maly, *Rechtsphilosophie* (Wien/New York 2001), p. 11.
24 G.C.J.J. van den Bergh, *Eigendom*, (Deventer 1988), p. 2; M. Kriechbaum, *Actio, ius und dominium in den Rechtslehren des 13. und 14. Jahrhunderts* (Ebelsbach 1996); review of this book: R. Feenstra, 'Dominium utile est chimaera: nouvelles réflexions sur le concept de propriété dans le droit savant (à propos d'un ouvrage récent)', *Tijdschrift voor Rechtsgeschiedenis* LXVI (1998), pp. 381–397.
25 It is striking that a philosophy of the law of succession and its links with the ancient ideas of family property is hardly ever developed.
26 C. 2,9 (10), 3, C. 1,18,1, C. 1,18,7. and C 1,18,6. These texts have influenced art. 2052 of the French Civil Code: 'Les transactions ont, entre parties, l'autorité de la chose jugée en dernier ressort. Elles ne peuvent être attaquées pour cause d'erreur de droit, ni pour cause de lésion.'
27 See Laurens Winkel, 'L'erreur de droit dans les procédures classiques et postclassiques romaines et l'histoire des articles 1356 e t 2052 du Code civil', *Tijdschrift voor Rechtsgeschiedenis* LIV (1985), pp. 321-332, esp. 324 ff.
28 D. Liebs, 'Die Herkunft der Regel "Bis de eadem re ne sit actio"', *Zeitschrift der Savigny Stiftung für Rechtsgeschichte*, rom. Abt. 84 (1967), p. 104 ff.

tions' of his predecessor Maurice Hauriou.[29] The underlying principle remains that lapse of time creates not only facts, but eventually also legal rules and principles. More recently, Jeremy Waldron and Tyler Cowen have argued, for different reasons, for the 'supersession' of historic injustice in some cases. Waldron has argued that restitution claims may become obsolete when circumstances change. For example, Waldron mentions the circumstance of more people coming in the world, calling for a new distribution of property rights. In line with Waldron, Cowen has emphasized the impossibility to evaluate hypothetical counterfactual ('what if') scenarios in most cases of historic injustice.[30]

A final remark about the relation of prescription with human rights and international law. According to a recent judgment of the European Court of Human Rights of 15 November 2005 there can be an interference of human rights and private law rules of prescription. In this judgement, the rules of adverse possession, according to English property law, causing an owner to lose his claim against someone who occupied his territory, are considered to be an infringement of the First Protocol protecting property, art. 1.[31] Other aspects of international law, such as prize law, do not seem to have been touched by the new developments of restitution. Eventually changes in prize law and in the rules concerning spoliation can be anticipated.

The chapters in this book have been presented as papers on an international conference held at Erasmus University Rotterdam on April 26, 2006. Finally, we thank all those who have collaborated to bring about the present versions of the articles, particularly Mrs. Tineke van de Pas-Van Hagen, Erasmus University Rotterdam, and Manon Tan, Irma Bluijs and Hjalmar Duin, student assistants at the Department of Legal Theory and Legal History, VU University Amsterdam.

December 2010

---

29 P. Hébraud, 'Observations sur la notion du temps dans le droit civil', in: *Études offertes à P. Kayser T. II* (Aix/ Marseilles 1979), pp. 1-58, esp. 50 ff.; cf. A. Brimo, 'Réflexions sur le temps dans la théorie générale du droit et de l'état', in: *Mélanges P. Hébraud* (Toulouse 1981), pp. 145-164; see also F. Ost, *Le temps du droit* (Paris 1999), pp. 136 ff.
30 See J. Waldron, 'Redressing Historic Injustice', *University of Toronto Law Journal* 52 (2005), pp. 135-160; T. Cowen, 'How Far Back Should We Go ? Why Restitution Should Be Small', in: J. Elster (ed.), *Retribution & Reparation in the Transition to Democracy* (Cambridge 2006), pp. 17-32.
31 J.A. Pye (Oxford) Ltd. v. United Kingdom [2005] ECHR 44302/02 (15 November 2005), see also A.C. van Schaick, *Nederlands Tijdschrift voor Burgerlijk Recht* (2006), pp. 90-94.

Post-war Restitution *vs* Present-day Reparation in France
Towards the Disappearance of Legal and Political Dilemmas?

Claire ANDRIEU (Paris)

It may sound paradoxical to focus on the dilemmas of post-war restitution of property rights since this policy was part of the process of re-establishing the rule of law after the Liberation of France in 1944. But the advantage of carrying out this critical analysis is that it highlights the main factors driving the policy implemented, as well as the factors of resistance against it. In so doing, it provides a dynamic picture of the restitution process. X-rayed in that way, post-war restitution calls for a comparison with the reparation phase that started in the 1990s.

To begin with, we should recall the main features of the spoliation and restitution phases in France. The responsibility for spoliation was shared by the Germans and the Vichy government (referred to here as the 'French State'). In the occupied zone, the Germans looted some 38,000 apartments, took gold and assets deposited in safes, stole artworks and imposed fines of 1 billion francs on Jews. The French State made provision for 'legal' spoliation of movable assets, stocks and shares, real estate and businesses.[1] The deportation of Jews went on from March 1942 to August 1944, with a quarter of the Jews residing in France at the time being sent to their deaths.

Three quarters of these Jews were alive when the Liberation took place: this is probably the main reason for the relatively good restitution rate achieved in the 1950s (about 90% of the value of real estate, businesses and bank and savings accounts).[2] The French part of the restitution process lasted for about ten years, and was followed by the German part, which lasted from the 1950s to the 1970s. Regarding the French side of the question, it may seem strange that this took more than twice as long as the spoliation. The reasons for this were both political and legal. Whereas spoliation was at the heart of Nazi policy and – to a lesser degree – that of the Vichy Government, restitution was not among the re-established Republic's most pressing priorities. It was certainly an imperative, but economic reconstruction and civil peace were considered to be far more urgent matters. Economic policy and budgetary issues sometimes conflicted with restitution. Moreover, the restoration of civil liberties and the rule of law enabled some of those who had acquired Jewish assets to slow down the whole process. But a long-lasting restitution process can also be in the victims'

---

[1] Loi du 22 juillet 1941 relative aux entreprises, biens et valeurs appartenant aux juifs, *Journal officiel de l'Etat Français,* 26 août 1941.
[2] Mission d'étude sur la spoliation des Juifs de France, *Rapport général* (Paris 2000), pp. 166-167.

interest. For instance, the time limit for filing a claim for reimbursement of the fines imposed by the Germans on Jews was deferred several times in the years before November 1951. The time limit on spoliations in Alsace-Moselle, which had been annexed by the Third Reich, was deferred until March 1953 or even, in certain cases, until December 1958.[3] These delays were designed to protect the rights of late claimants. Restitution takes a lot longer to accomplish than spoliation. One is not the contrary of the other: they are not symmetrical processes.

The 1944 'Bill of Rights' encountered legal and political dilemmas

On what grounds could the principle of restitution possibly conflict with Republican law? The quickest way to return the assets would have been to spoliate the spoliators. In 1917, in keeping with communist ideology against private ownership of property, the Soviets adopted a revolutionary stance of this kind, breaking all international economic contracts and political treaties in doing so. Refusing to acknowledge any of the previous regime's commitments, they stopped, for instance, making payments on 'Russian loans'. These were not repaid until after 1989. Legally, De Gaulle's government could have acted in the same way. As early as August 1940, De Gaulle had declared anti-Semitic policy "null and void". Any subsequent law spoliating the spoliators would not have been retroactive as the policy itself was declared invalid by Free France. Through various declarations, Free France had made it clear that it recognised only Republican law and no other. Furthermore, in April 1941, the spoliators had been duly warned in a BBC Free French broadcast that all confiscations were "null and void" and that "the last owner will not be allowed to claim any compensation." The Inter-Allied Declaration of January 1943 gave a similar warning.[4] In November 1943, the French Committee for National Liberation had adopted a restitution edict in Algiers. The 9 August 1944 Act, which was also signed in Algiers

---

3   "Modalités de remboursement des prélèvements exercés sur les avoirs des personnes spoliées", Arrêté du ministre des finances et des affaires économiques, 29 septembre 1951, *Journal officiel de la République française (JORF)*, 4 octobre 1951 ; "Remboursement des prélèvements exercés par l'ennemi sur les avoirs des personnes spoliées", arrêté du secrétaire d'Etat aux finances, 11 octobre 1952, *JORF*, 15 octobre 1952 ; Arrêté du 17 juillet 1958 portant fixation d'un délai pour le dépôt des demandes d'indemnités de dépossession ou de reconstitution dues pour spoliation, *JORF*, 25 juillet 1958. All legal texts (French and German) relating to anti-Semitic spoliations and restitutions in France can be found on the CD Rom accompanying the collection: C. Andrieu et al. (eds.), *La persécution des Juifs de France, 1940-1944, et le rétablissement de la légalité républicaine*, Mission d'étude sur la spoliation des Juifs de France (Paris 2000).

4   C. Andrieu, supported by C. Omnès et al., *La Spoliation financière*, Mission d'étude sur la spoliation des Juifs de France (Paris 2000), pp. 71-72.

and "related to the re-establishing of Republican law on the continental territory," stated that:[5]

> Article 1: The form of the Government of France is and remains the Republic. By law the latter has never ceased to exist.
> Article 2: Are consequently null and of no effect all acts [...] promulgated on the continental territory after 16 June 1940 [...].
> Article 3: Is expressly stated the nullity of the following acts:
> [...]
> All those that establish or enforce any discrimination based on the quality of being Jewish.
> [...].

This solemn proclamation in 1944 contributed to de-legitimising any attempt to resist restitution and indeed played a symbolic part in speeding up restitution. The main order, which was passed on 21 April 1945 and related to the nullity of spoliation acts, followed from the 1944 declaration of principles.[6] René Cassin, a law professor who had been De Gaulle's legal advisor from the beginning of Free France, played a decisive role in this 1945 order. When France was liberated, De Gaulle appointed him head of the Conseil d'Etat, the supreme administrative court. The 1945 order declared all private buyers of Jewish businesses or real estate to be 'bad faith' owners and considered all contracts signed by persons deemed to be Jewish since June 1940 as having been concluded under duress. In the event of dispute, the burden of proof was on the acquirer. With a view to accelerating the return of the assets, the order also stated that the nullity of all sales accomplished under the Occupation should be certified through an emergency judicial procedure known as the '*référé*', instead of going through the traditional civil courts route. That year, thousands of *référés* were speeded up.

Nevertheless, the preamble to the 1944 declaration specified that "considerations of practical interest recommended avoiding a return, without transition, to the state of law in force on the foresaid date of 16 June 1940." The text considered enforcing a "transitory period of time" and, "even the definitive validation of certain acquired situations whose reversal would cause more considerable trouble to the country than their confirmation." In the case of restitution, this meant that the spoliators would not be abruptly spoliated, but instead legally dispossessed.

---

5 Ordonnance du 9 août 1944 relative au rétablissement de la légalité républicaine sur le territoire continental, *JORF*, 10 août 1944.

6 Ordonnance du 21 avril 1945 portant deuxième application de l'ordonnance du 12 novembre 1943 sur la nullité des actes de spoliation accomplis par l'ennemi ou sous son contrôle, et édictant la restitution aux victimes de ces actes de ceux de leurs biens qui ont fait l'objet d'actes de disposition, *JORF*, 23 avril 1945.

Paradoxically, other legal principles, such as liberty and equality, may have conflicted with the restitution process. In order, for instance, to repress the beginnings of a resistance to restitution, the freedom of association had to be limited. An edict dated 31 December 1944 restrained this liberty by forbidding any voluntary organization "whose activity would tend to foil the dispositions related to the re-establishment of Republican law."[7] The preamble stated in plain language:

> Thanks to the return of civil liberties, groups or associations have formed in order to foil the implementation of orders taken to re-establish republican law.
> In particular, groups which intend to defend the profiteers of the racist legislation have not been afraid to create associations declared under the regime of the 1 July 1901 law.
> In order to have such manoeuvres stopped and to avoid the slowness of the judicial procedure without suppressing the guarantees resulting from jurisdictional control, [...].

The principle of equality before the law could also slow down restitution by preventing the law from establishing a hierarchy among war victims, even if some of them had been more severely affected than others. The 16 October 1944 order, for instance, relating to the restitution of certain assets sequestered by the *Administration des Domaines* (State Property Department) listed 32 types of sequestration.[8] The sequestration of Jewish assets was only one of these, and no priority was given to any of the 32. In some cases, competition between victims turned out to favour conventional war victims. An order dated 14 November 1944 tried to address the question of enabling tenants who had fled into hiding during the occupation to return to their former homes,[9] but the devastation caused by the war, mostly by bombs, had razed 460,000 buildings to the ground and damaged two million others. Disaster victims, evacuees and refugees of all sorts had been rehoused in vacant apartments, requisitioned for that purpose. "In this exceptional case" – which in fact was not rare – the former tenant, who was most often Jewish, had to wait until the new occupier could find another place to live. In this particular situation, the right of first occupier was provisionally, therefore, given to conventional war victims rather than to those who had escaped round-ups and deportation to death camps.

---

7 Ordonnance du 30 décembre 1944 portant modification de la loi du 10 janvier 1936 sur les groupes de combat et milices privées [itself modifying the law dated 1 July 1901 relating to the contract of association], *JORF*, 31 décembre 1944.

8 Ordonnance du 16 octobre 1944 relative à la restitution par l'administration des Domaines de certains biens mis sous séquestre, *JORF*, 16 et 17 octobre 1944.

9 Ordonnance du 14 novembre 1944 concernant la réintégration de certains locataires, *JORF*, 15 novembre 1944.

Another reason for the relative slowness of restitution lies in the inadequacies of corrective justice at a national and international level. In France, the buyers of Jewish businesses and real estate had already been declared 'bad faith' owners. But while the *référé* immediately gave property rights back to the legitimate owner, there were occasional disputes about the figures contained in the balance sheets accompanying the spoliated goods that buyers handed back to victims. In other cases, acquirers would try to demonstrate their good faith. Since the rule of law had been re-established, these arguments could result in trials. But, until 1949, the most disturbing element of the restitution process was the absence of one of the main aryanizers: the German State. France had to resort to internal distributive justice: the 1946 war damages law included furniture stolen by the Germans in its list of indemnifications, while a 1948 budgetary law stipulated that the fine levied by the occupier would be reimbursed by the French Treasury.[10] The same endorsement by French law and the budget was adopted in 1949 for all spoliations committed in respect of Jewish and non-Jewish assets in Alsace-Moselle.[11] The procedure regarding gold was even slower. This relied on the 1946 Paris Inter-Allied Agreement and required negotiations between the Allies. In France, reimbursement was a two-stage operation, beginning in 1953 and ending in 1958.[12] On top of these delays, a legal obstacle was often imposed on non-French Jews if their country of origin was declared an 'enemy'. Although 'enemy' or stateless citizens were often refugees from Nazi countries, they were sometimes prevented from benefiting from some of the French laws and decrees in cases where compensation in France came through a State process. Although ministerial circulars progressively removed legal barriers for refugees, 'enemy' victims often had a hard time recovering their assets.

Political views at the time, shared by 80% of the French electorate, could also hinder the restitution process. In 1944-1946, polls, electoral results and parliamentary votes showed a quasi-unanimity in favour of

---

10 Loi du 28 octobre 1946 sur les dommages de guerre, *JORF,* 29 octobre 1946 ; loi du 16 juin 1948 portant aménagements fiscaux, *JORF,* 17 juin 1948.
11 Loi du 23 avril 1949 portant application des articles 7 et 16 de l'ordonnance du 21 avril 1945 sur la nullité des actes de spoliation accomplis par l'ennemi ou sous son contrôle, et de l'article 6 de la loi du 28 octobre 1946 sur les dommages de guerre, *JORF,* 24 avril 1949.
12 Avis du 16 mai 1953 relatif à l'attribution aux personnes ayant subi des spoliations d'or d'une partie de l'or reçu par la France de la commission internationale de l'or monétaire créée par l'accord de Paris sur les réparations, *JORF,* 16 mai 1953 ; avis du 10 octobre 1958 relatif à une attribution complémentaire d'or monétaire aux personnes qui, ayant subi des spoliations d'or, ont bénéficié de l'attribution d'une partie de l'or reçu par la France de la commission internationale de l'or monétaire créée par l'accord de Paris sur les réparations, *JORF,* 10 octobre 1958.

nationalizations.¹³ State ownership was considered part of the 'social and economic democracy' that was to be set up at the Liberation, according to the programme of the National Council of the Resistance. This new vision of economic policy could not but affect the return to private property rights. Artworks seized in Germany in 1945, for example, that remained unclaimed in the following years were either sold by the State or placed in the custody of national museums in 1954. That specific measure was not regarded as theft at the time, as it would tend to be nowadays, but instead as a democratic measure. Another striking example of this state-inclined spirit can be found in the great restitution order of 21 April 1945. Whereas private buyers of Jewish assets were declared 'bad faith' owners, Article 15 of this order stipulated that the order was not applicable if the State had acquired the properties in pursuit of its pre-emptive right. The same Article 15 allowed retrocession, but only through a heavy and slow procedure that required the advice of the *Conseil d'Etat*. As late as December 1953, a decree set out the exact procedures to be followed by dispossessed proprietors wanting to get real estate back that had been assigned to a ministry.¹⁴

All these loopholes in the provisions representing the 1944 declaration of principles ended up by creating an obstacle to restitution in certain cases. On the whole, their cumulative effect remained quantitatively marginal, as we have seen, but some dispossessed individuals may have felt very differently.

Present-day reparation policy: the advantages of de-contextualization

In France, a reparation policy (as opposed to a restitution policy) was initiated in 1997 to complete the process of restitution. However, the present policy can hardly be regarded as a resumption and continuation of its predecessor.¹⁵ This marks a radical change from the post-war context. Because the Shoah has come to epitomise Evil, public policy can now focus on this category of war victims without appearing to deviate from the principle of equality before the law in financial matters. Restitution is now seen

---

13 C. Andrieu, L. Le Van & A. Prost (eds.), *Les nationalisations de la Libération. De l'utopie au compromis* (Paris 1987).
14 Décret du 23 décembre 1953 relatif à la rétrocession aux personnes spoliées des immeubles réquisitionnés en propriété, expropriés ou acquis par l'Etat, en vertu de son droit de préemption et de priorité, pendant l'occupation allemande, *JORF,* 29 décembre 1953.
15 For a global comparison, see C. Andrieu, 'En France, deux cycles de politique publique : restitutions (1944-1954) et réparations (1997-…)', in: C. Goschler, Ph. Ther & C. Andrieu (eds.), *Spoliation et restitution des biens juifs en Europe au XX° siècle* (Paris 2007), revised and augmented edition of C. Goschler & Ph. Ther (eds.), *Raub und Restitution* (Franfurt am Main 2003). English edition: M. Dean, C. Goshler & Ph. Ther (eds.), *Robbery and Restitution, The Conflict over Jewish Property in Europe* (New York 2007), pp. 134-154.

as a form of moral reparation rather than a mere return of assets to legitimate owners. Moreover, the country is prosperous and the political environment is much more market-friendly than it used to be. While a new vision of the past is emerging, most of the grounds for the post-war dilemmas have now disappeared. The end of the Cold War also highlighted the absence of restitution in ex-communist countries and, as an indirect consequence, Western media launched inquiries into what had happened with regard to restitution in their own countries.

The main characteristics of the present situation are having an effect on the legal proceedings for reparation. In particular, the respective shares of corrective and distributive justice have changed since the post-war era. The principle of corrective justice now targets financial institutions, along with museums. After the war, the State did not trouble insurance companies and banks about assets, such as unclaimed life insurance policies or accounts, held in victims' names.[16] Immediately after the liberation of Paris, Jews were given free and immediate access to their bank and savings accounts.[17] But no systematic searches were carried out for the heirs of unclaimed life insurance policies and dormant accounts. As far as bank accounts and savings were concerned, the thirty-year statute of limitation meant that any amounts owed to these heirs would eventually be paid to the State. But this policy was reversed in the 1990s. Intervention by the United States in European restitution policy – a novelty compared with the post-war years, at least as far as France was concerned – included threats to close the American market to European companies if they failed to comply with American demands. Economic globalization allowed class actions to exert real pressure on these companies. This is why financial institutions form a separate case within France's present system of reparations. Private and state-owned banks paid their own share of such amounts to the Foundation for the memory of the Shoah created in 2000.[18] They paid up to 40% of the total funds, with the other 60% being paid by the State. They are also paying individual claims presented to the ICHEIC (International Commission on Holocaust-Era Insurance Claims) or to the French Commission for the Compensation of Victims of Spoliation (CIVS), which was established in 1999.[19] Until 2005, payments by banks represented 9% of all individual

---

16 Andrieu et al., *La Spoliation financière*.
17 Le Secrétaire général aux Finances, lettre au président de l'Association professionnelle des banques, 30 août 1944, vol. 2, p. 113.
18 Décret du 26 décembre 2000 portant reconnaissance d'une fondation comme établissement d'utilité publique, *JORF*, 30 décembre 2000.
19 Décret du 10 septembre 1999 instituant une commission pour l'indemnisation des victimes de spoliations intervenues du fait des législations antisémites en vigueur pendant l'Occupation, *JORF*, 11 septembre 1999.

compensation paid through the CIVS, [20] with the remaining 91% being paid by the State.

The share of compensation now endorsed by the State (60% of collective reparations and 91% of individual payments) significantly exceeds its financial participation in post-war restitution. This change results from the French State's acknowledgement in 1995 of collective responsibility for the deportation of the Jews. The disproportionate share of distributive justice in the present reparation cycle also reflects the political and practical choice – sixty years after the events – not to search for buyers of Jewish assets. The estimated value of businesses and real estate that was not restituted to the victims represents 55% of the State payments to the Foundation's funds, and 25% of the State's payments of individual claims, whereas in the post-war years the buyers themselves had to return assets to their rightful owners. As compensation, they were given back the amount they had paid for the specific assets. These amounts were deposited in an account in the Jewish owner's name at a state-owned bank, the *Caisse des dépôts et consignations*. Since the buyers of Jewish assets or indeed the professional organizations that participated in the process of spoliation are no longer being sought under the present reparation system, both of these groups are benefiting from preferential treatment compared to that applied to depositary institutions. Consequently, the current system does not fully guarantee equality of treatment of the various parties involved in spoliation. The situation is very different, therefore, from the period immediately following the war: nowadays, it is the State and financial institutions that are being targeted for reparations rather than the private individuals or businesses that bought Jewish assets.

Another fundamental change in legal practice was necessary in order to re-open the restitution file. All statutes of limitation have now been removed. This is why the CIVS is not a regular court of law, but instead a 'commission' which issues 'recommendations'. It judges 'in equity', and its decisions, deprived of any legal status, are obeyed by the government, banks and insurance companies. This procedure differs sharply from the legalistic one followed immediately after the war. From a legal point of view, the CIVS is an exceptional court. The legal system does not usually appreciate exceptions to the rule. However, although alien to the legal tradition, this procedure may be the best way to deal with an exceptional, almost unique situation from the past. The fact that other war victims, specifically the thousands of people whose houses were bombed, have not called for a similar removing of the statutes of limitation shows that public opinion is now able to accept a certain inequality of treatment among war victims. In the case, however, of individual pensions, the deportees of the Resistance claimed, and in 2004 obtained, equality of treatment with the

---

20 CIVS, *Annual report*, 31 December 2005.

provisions established when the law was revised in 2000 in favour of orphans of Jewish deportees.[21]

Apart from these changes, there remains a strong continuity between both cycles: just like restitution, reparation is based on a historical study of the file on each asset. Whenever possible, spoliation and post-war restitution archives are searched for and then closely studied. There is no limit on the total amount of individual compensation, except in the case of bank and savings accounts, where compensation depends on an inter-governmental agreement reached in January 2001 between France and the United States.[22] This agreement is the result of the pressure exerted by two class actions filed in New York against French banks. The agreement creates a breach in the French system by allowing a lump sum to be distributed to claimants without documentary evidence and where the archives do not show any trace of an account. Apart from this exception, the reparation system functions just like after the Liberation, without a market built on settlements and lawyers' fees, while being free of charge for the claimant and based on historical facts.

Today, fact-finding procedures remain the basic principle on which reparation is founded, as was the case for restitution. But the reparation cycle appeals to 'equity' and includes a touch of bargaining filtered through an international agreement, whereas the post-war cycle was purely a legal process. Both approaches have included a mix of corrective and distributive justice, even if the proportion changed in favour of the latter in the 1990s. As the legal, economic and political constraints of the post-war period have disappeared, present-day reparation policy has far fewer dilemmas to resolve. It has been de-contextualized, except for the memory of the Shoah, which is and will undoubtedly remain a vibrant and driving force for the whole process.

---

21 Décret du 13 juillet 2000 instituant une mesure de réparation pour les orphelins dont les parents ont été victimes de persécutions antisémites, *JORF*, 14 juillet 2000 ; décret du 27 juillet 2004 instituant une aide financière en reconnaissance des souffrances endurées par les orphelins dont les parents ont été victimes d'actes de barbarie durant la Deuxième Guerre mondiale, *JORF*, 29 juillet 2004.

22 Décret du 21 mars 2001 portant publication de l'accord entre le Gouvernement de la République française et le Gouvernement des Etats-Unis d'Amérique relatif à l'indemnisation de certaines spoliations intervenues pendant la Seconde Guerre mondiale (ensemble trois annexes et un échange de notes), signé à Washington le 18 janvier 2001, *JORF*, 23 mars 2001.

Contrasting legal concepts of restitution in France and the Netherlands (1943-1952)

Wouter VERAART (Amsterdam)

In this article[*] I would like to explore the following thesis: how is it possible that the process of post-war restitution of property rights in the Netherlands was characterized by extreme pragmatism, while in France the same process complied much more with formal principles of legality and the rule of law? Or, to put it differently, how is it possible that the Dutch used open-ended legal rules and a special court of restoration, equipped with large discretionary powers, while the French, by contrast, applied strict rules and normal courts, with little freedom of decision? Furthermore, how is it possible that the interests of the Dutch administration clashed with the interests of the post-war Jewish community during the process of restitution, while the French administration expended considerable efforts to make sure that Jewish owners were really getting their assets back? And how is it possible that the heroes of the French restitution process, René Cassin and Émile Terroine, were distinguished members of the De Gaulle administration, while the hero of the Dutch restitution process, Heiman Sanders, was a lonely lawyer on the side of the decimated Dutch Jewish community? Let's finish these opening questions by asking a final one: how is it possible that recent evaluations of the Dutch restitution process have tended to be very critical, while the evaluation of the post-war restitution process in France – by the Mattéoli commission in April 2000 – has been summarized in one sentence:

"On the whole, the restored French Republic did its duty."[1]

My main explanation for this is that there was a big difference in vision on the restitution process in both countries. Within French political circles, the restitution of looted property was considered as a necessary step within the project of re-establishing legality and the rule of law, while the Dutch government considered the restitution process primarily as just one of the

---

[*] This article is a more detailed version of a lecture he gave on 30 December 2002 at the International Conference on Confronting History: The Historical Commissions of Inquiry, at Yad Vashem, Jerusalem.

[1] *Summary of the work by the Study Mission on the spoliation of Jews in France* (Mission Mattéoli) (Paris 2000), p.12. This summary is available on the Documentation Française website: www.ladocfrancaise.gouv.fr. The report of the Mission itself consists of several volumes (including a general report), which are also published by the Documentation Française.

exceptional measures and policies necessary for the economic reconstruction of the country.

Spoliation (1940-1945)

In my opinion, appreciating this difference in vision may help us to better understand and evaluate the process of restitution in the two countries during the years 1945-1952. A comparison between the French and Dutch approaches does not seem out of place as there are many similarities in the historical and legal backgrounds of their restitution operations. Firstly, the Dutch and French legal systems belong to the same legal family: the continental Roman law system. Moreover, the French Civil Code of 1804 had a major influence on the conception of the Dutch Civil Code of 1838. Apart from some dogmatic differences, both countries have most of their fundamental legal principles in common. Secondly, the histories of the spoliation of the Jews in both countries show some striking similarities. Both countries were at least partly occupied. In both countries the systems of spoliation were to a large degree legalized. In the legalization of the process, the Vichy government was even more orthodox than the German military authorities in the French occupied zone,[2] while in the Netherlands the German occupation took on a civilian form. Between 1940 and 1943, the *Reichskommissar* of the Dutch occupied territories, Seyss-Inquart, a skilled Austrian jurist, issued thirteen decrees specifically designed to deprive Jews in the Netherlands of more or less all their assets: not only their movable and unmovable assets, but also all kinds of financial rights, such as securities, mortgages, insurance policies and claims against third parties. In this spoliation process, the Germans used different institutions ('looting institutions', as they were later called) to deprive the Jewish population of their rights, with the most notorious institution using the same abbreviated name ('Liro') as that of the Jewish bank Lippmann, Rosenthal & Co., Sarphatistraat. Jews were obliged to deposit all their assets at this institution. Liro then sold these assets without the permission of the former owners. Renowned Dutch institutions, such as the Dutch central bank, which was controlled by the Germans during the war, and the Dutch Stockbrokers' Association, collaborated with Liro in this process. The Stockbrokers' Association even took the initiative by asking the German authorities for permission for the Jewish securities to be sold on the Amsterdam Stock Exchange. The Association received a positive reply and admitted Liro to its membership and hence to dealings on the stock exchange, while a large proportion of its members were actively involved in trading Jewish securities. Liro did not keep the profits from these sales;

---

2   *Summary of the work by the Study Mission on the spoliation of Jews in France*, p. 21.

instead these went to another German 'looting institution', the *Vermögensverwaltungs- und Rentenanstalt* ('VVRA').[3]

The 'success' of the looting operation in the Netherlands is reflected in the fact that only some 30,000 Dutch Jews (according to German definitions) survived the war. More than 100,000 were deported and murdered. The spoliation in the Netherlands consequently exceeded the spoliation in France in both breadth and depth. In France, the spoliation did not cover the entire spectrum of rights: there was no *systematic* spoliation, for example, of insurance policies and mortgages. Furthermore, the spoliation in France took place at a slower pace than in the Netherlands. The 'aryanization' of Jewish enterprises by the notorious General Commission of Jewish Affairs (a subdepartment of the Vichy administration), for example, was carried out strictly in compliance with legal forms; specific 'looting institutions', such as Liro in the Netherlands, did not exist.[4] The report of the French Mattéoli commission refers to "the inherent slowness *à la française*" of the administration, which was extremely bureaucratic. It is significant, in this regard, that Vichy-France tried to use the aryanization of Jewish enterprises as a means of fostering French economic interests rather than as an end in itself.[5]

The aryanization process was far from complete by the time of the liberation. The percentage of unfinished files (concerning assets, businesses and property holdings still under administration and not yet liquidated or sold) varied from 53% in the Seine region to approximately 60% in the south.[6] These facts are reflected in the fact that the number of Jews in France who survived the war was much higher than in the Netherlands, both in relative and absolute terms.[7]

Notwithstanding the differences in the breadth and depth of the spoliation in both countries, the basic elements are similar. The main objective was to deprive part of the population of their rights (primarily, but not only, Jews), to outlaw them on a racial basis and to damage them in their capacities as legal subjects and citizens. As Raul Hilberg has shown, the expropriation of the Jews was a necessary step in the process of annihilating

---

[3] See W.J. Veraart, *Deprivation and restitution of property rights during the years of occupation and post-war reconstruction in the Netherlands and in France* (in Dutch) (Deventer 2005), pp. 74-75.

[4] See Jean-Marc Dreyfus, 'Die Enteignung der Juden in Westeuropa', in: Constantin Goschler and Philipp Ther (ed.), *Raub und Restitution. 'Arisierung' und Rückerstattung des jüdischen Eigentums in Europa* (Frankfurt am Main 2003), pp. 51-52.

[5] *Summary of the work by the Study Mission on the spoliation of Jews in France*, p. 21. See also Philippe Verheyde, *Les mauvais comptes de Vichy. L'aryanisation des entreprises juives* (Paris 1999), pp. 30-31.

[6] *Summary of the work by the Study Mission on the spoliation of Jews in France*, p. 22.

[7] See Dreyfus, 'Die Enteignung der Juden in Westeuropa', p. 42.

European Jewry.[8] The term 'spoliation' does not capture this point very well: in my opinion it wrongly suggests that greed or profit-seeking were its driving forces. This was certainly not the case, as shown by the fact that the 'looting' operation was utterly democratic in its targets: it hit rich and poor alike.

Joint Declaration of St James (5 January 1943)

To return to the basic question: why was the process of post-war restitution of property rights in the Netherlands characterized by an extreme pragmatism, while in France this very same process complied much more with formal principles of legality and the rule of law? I have pointed out that the French and Dutch legal systems shared (and share), to a large degree, the same fundamental legal principles, and that both countries faced a similar massive deprivation of the rights of one part of their populations. But there are even more similarities. A few days after the German invasion of the Netherlands on 10 May 1940, the Head of State, Queen Wilhelmina, fled to Britain and the Dutch cabinet followed her into exile. During the war the Dutch government stayed in London and spent much of its time preparing for return. Meanwhile, on 18 June 1940, the French General Charles De Gaulle responded to the 'armistice' of Pétain by his famous 'appel' from London and appointed himself Leader of the Free French. As the war went on (and the name of his movement changed) De Gaulle's leadership became more and more legalized and embedded in institutions. Some of the French civilians who rallied behind him became commissioners of the French National Committee (established in September 1941) presided over by De Gaulle.

On 5 January 1943, seventeen allied governments (including the Dutch government-in-exile) and the French National Committee solemnly proclaimed the Joint Declaration, in which they issued a formal warning:

> "to all concerned [...] that they intended to do their utmost to defeat the methods of dispossession practised by the Governments with which they are at war [...]."

They reserved:

> "all their rights to declare invalid any transfers of, or dealings with property, rights and interests of any description whatsoever which are, or have been situated in the territories which have come under occupation or control [...] of the Governments with which they are at war [...]."

---

8   See Raul Hilberg, *The Destruction of the European Jews*, Revised and Definitive Edition (New York 1985), chapter III.

This warning applied:

> "whether such transfers or dealings have taken the form of open looting or plunder, or of transactions apparently legal in form, even when they purport to be voluntarily effected."[9]

The Joint Declaration of January 1943 may be seen as a common starting point in the history of the post-war restitution process in both the Netherlands and France.[10] But these open-ended formulations could hardly provide a basis for real guidelines, and the Allies did not do much to harmonize their drafts of legal measures more or less 'based' upon it.

Preparing for post-war restitution in the Netherlands (1943-1945)

How did the French and the Dutch prepare for post-war restitution as promised in the Joint Declaration? Let's discuss the Dutch preparation first. The Joint Declaration was mentioned in a Dutch radio broadcast from London on 7 January 1943. Nevertheless, it does not seem to have played an important role during the Dutch government's preparation of the post-war restoration of the country. Towards the end of 1942, the preparation of decrees concerning 'the restoration of legal relations' was assigned to a small committee presided over by a civil law professor, Jannes Eggens. The other members were civil servants, two of whom were Dutch Jews. Eggens was a renowned academic with strong but controversial views on the role of law in society. Under his influence the committee decided that the violations and corruptions of legal relations under German occupation had been so diverse and complex that they could only be repaired on the basis of 'common sense' in a very flexible, pragmatic way. The judge had to apply open standards of 'equity' and 'reasonableness' within the special circumstances of each specific case. If a transaction was based on racist legislation retroactively declared null and void by the Dutch government (as it did in its E93 decree on 17 September 1944), the annulment of the transaction was presumed to be reasonable, although not obligatory. Judges were not supposed to behave like jurists, but like 'good men' or 'arbitrators'. The possibility of appeal or cassation was excluded, not only to speed up the process, but also to prevent too much legal discussion. Eggens' draft also provided some

---

9   This declaration was repeated in July 1944, in part VI of the Bretton Woods Declaration.
10 It is important to note, however, that the Joint Declaration was primarily drafted as a warning to neutral states, such as Switzerland and Sweden, not to profit from all kinds of spoliation of the Germans in the occupied territories. Its main purpose was to protect the national interests of the Allied states, much more than the particular interests of individual victims. The spoliation of the Jews was not explicitly mentioned in the Joint Declaration.

rules to protect the recipients of despoiled property against claims from the former owners. They could keep the property if they made a reasonable case that they acquired it in good faith. The committee also offered protection to people who, under influence of German regulations, 'paid off' the debts they owed to Jewish creditors to non-Jewish institutions or people, for example to Liro. These protective measures in favour of third persons went much further than the protection offered to third parties in normal Dutch civil law and became a cause of distress among the dispossessed Jewish community after the war.

Although the Eggens Committee provided some specific information on the spoliation of Dutch Jews, its primary mission was to restore the Dutch legal system to a healthy state, rather than provide a principled response to the deprivation of the rights of one part of the population. Eggens believed that the exceptional situation caused by the German occupation could only be undone by an exceptional institution, equipped with exceptional powers. This became the Council of Restoration of Rights ('Council of Restoration', which operated from 1945 to 1967). In its final form, the Council of Restoration was divided in four divisions: a Judicial Division, an Administration Division, an Immovable Property Division and a Securities Division. The Judicial Division was the only independent division. The others received instructions from different members of the government. This dependency was inconsistent with the separation of powers, as the non-judicial divisions could take binding decisions in disputes about looted property (with appeal to the Judicial Division). Under the Dutch constitution, only the independent judiciary is entitled to decide on property disputes. Eggens, however, believed that this departure from the constitution had to be tolerated for practical reasons.[11]

In the post-war period (1945-1952), the Dutch Minister of Finance, Lieftinck, got a strong hold on the non-judicial divisions of the Council of Restoration. He used the restitution machinery mainly to pursue the financial interests of the Dutch State (in order to reconstruct the economy), even if this policy conflicted with the interests of the dispossessed Jewish community. He often claimed that the Dutch State could not in any way be held responsible for the spoliation of the Jews. This position was hard to maintain when it became clear that renowned Dutch institutions, such as the Central Bank and the Stockbrokers' Association, had collaborated with the Germans in the process of spoliation. But Lieftinck never changed his opinion and did everything he could to protect Dutch financial institutions such as these against claims during the post-war period. As a result, the only

---

11 The Dutch Decree on the restoration of legal relations ('*Besluit Herstel Rechtsverkeer*', *Staatsblad* E100) was promulgated on September 17, 1944 and changed by Decree F272, on November 16, 1945. For more details, see Veraart, *Ontrechting en rechtsherstel*, pp. 63-67.

institution trusted by the Jewish community became the independent Judicial Division of the Council of Restoration.

With respect to looted securities, virtually nothing happened until 1952 because the Securities Division blocked restitution to the former owners. A breakthrough became possible in 1953, after a sensational judgment by the independent Judicial Division and Lieftinck's departure as Minister. In June 1953, the government, the Stockbrokers' Association and representatives of the Jewish community, reached an out-of-court settlement. Former owners of looted securities that were sold by Liro on the Amsterdam Stock Exchange received compensation of 90% of the current value of their assets from the Dutch State.[12]

Preparing for post-war restitution in France (1943-1945)

In early 1945, a brilliant French professor of law, René Cassin, De Gaulle's main legal advisor, gave a lecture on the difficulties that De Gaulle and his movement experienced during the war:

> "While the governments of the Queen of the Netherlands, or of the King of Norway, could be recognized thanks to [the presence of] their sovereigns, we had no head of state, no legitimate chief of government in Great Britain. As a consequence, the institution representing France in the coalition of allies was incompletely recognized between June 1940 and October 1944."[13]

This 'political and legal handicap', as Cassin called it[14], was serious. For example, according to US president Roosevelt, De Gaulle's leadership lacked credibility and the president did not change his mind until very late in the war.[15] The Free French had to prove to the world that they were the only legitimate representatives of France. They fought this uphill battle for recognition on two fronts: on the one hand they were looking for support in the colonies and among the resistance movements in France, while on the other hand they set up a complex institutional framework that complied, as

---

12 Ibid., pp. 192-194; 200-204. See also *Eindrapport van de Begeleidingscommissie onderzoek financiële tegoeden WO-II in Nederland* (Scholten-Commission), Part II, 'Effecten' (Leiden, 15 December 1999), pp. 393-400 (available at www.minfin.nl).
13 Lecture of René Cassin 'sur les problèmes juridiques posés au Comité français et au Gouvernement provisoire par la poursuite de la guerre et la Libération', 21 March 1945, in: *Bulletin trimestriel de la société de Législation Comparée* (Paris, 1946 No. 1-2), p. 13: 'Tandis que le gouvernement de la reine des Pays-Bas ou du roi de Norvège avait la possibilité d'être reconnu aux côtés de son souverain, nous n'avions ni chef d'état ni chef de gouvernement en Angleterre. Par conséquent, l'institution qui représentait la France dans la coalition a été, de juin 1940 à octobre 1944, incomplètement reconnue.' (Translation by the author.)
14 Ibid.
15 See Simon Berthon, *Allies at War: The Bitter Rivalry among Churchill, Roosevelt, and De Gaulle* (New York 2001).

much as possible, with the best traditions of democracy and the rule of law traditions that Vichy had forsaken. A significant step in this regard was the establishment of the Provisional Advisory Assembly in October 1943.[16] This was a provisional parliament in which the populations of the colonies, resistance groups and victims of persecution were, more or less, represented. Cassin, who was an assimilated Jew himself, became chairman of two influential committees on legislation that were set up. As such he played a key role in preparing the French restitution laws.

The preparation of these laws was a complex and lengthy affair. To begin with, the French National Committee took the Joint Declaration of 7 January 1943 very seriously. Just a few weeks later it published another Free French declaration, which was directly based on it. The following major step was taken on 9 August 1944, when the Decree on the re-establishment of the republican legality was issued. This decree in principle invalidated all legal measures taken by the Germans or the Vichy authorities. Although the invalidation of concrete legal acts was generally postponed to a later date, section 3 mentioned a few categories of legal measures that were declared null and void from the outset, including "all [legal texts] which apply or enforce any sort of discrimination based upon the quality of being Jewish."[17]

It is the direct link between the re-establishment of the republican legality of France and the retroactive annulment of the unjust, racist legislation that interests me here. The Decree re-establishing the republican legality possessed an immediate practical relevance, but also had a very strong symbolic value. During the session of the Advisory Assembly on 26 June 1944, Cassin emphasized in his speech the "particular significance" of this decree "for the future, for the psychology, for the state of mind of our people."[18] In the same speech he stressed the importance of undoing the spoliation for the victims: "Returned to a liberated France, not one of them [Jews, patriots, Gaullists and others] would tolerate not being immediately reintegrated into

---

16 Lecture of René Cassin on 21 March 1945, pp. 15-16.
17 'Article 3: Est expressément constatée la nullité des actes suivants: [...] Tous ceux qui établissent ou appliquent une discrimination quelconque fondée sur la qualité de juif.' (Translation by the author). The legal texts published in the official French and German journals from 1940 to the present (both on the spoliation and on post-war restitution) have been collected in a single volume by the Documentation Française: *La persécution des Juifs de France (1940-1944) et le rétablissement de la légalité républicaine* (Paris 2000).
18 See 'Assemblée Consultative Provisoire. Séance du 26 Juin 1944' in: *Journal Officiel de la République Française* (Algiers, 29 June 1944), pp. 97-98: 'M. René Cassin, président de la commission de législation et de réforme de l'état: "[...] Mais, je le crois, cette ordonnance sur la légalité républicaine - qui est la première après l'ordonnance sur le rétablissement des pouvoirs publics - cette ordonnance a pour l'avenir, pour la psychologie, l'état d'esprit de notre peuple, une particulière signifiance."

his premises or his enterprise."[19] The same message could also be deduced from the system of the Decree itself: re-establishing the republican legality obviously meant annulling the unjust pseudo-legislation of Vichy. And this could only be realized by undoing the spoliation – the deprivation of rights of some parts of the population – in a principled, legal way.

At the time of liberation, the Decree re-establishing the republican legality was directly used to bring about restitutions. This mode of operation was sometimes very effective, although it was deemed to be inconvenient because the August 1944 Decree did not lay down any material or procedural rules with regard to the restitution of property, and it took a considerable amount of time for this legal gap to be filled. Following various decrees issued in November 1944, by far the most important piece of legislation was the decree issued on 21 April 1945. The long delay was partly due to a political struggle between the Department of Justice on the one hand, and the commissions on legislation, the Advisory Assembly and certain organizations of Jewish victims of persecution on the other. In contrast to the Dutch situation, where far fewer Jews had survived the war and those who had survived were hardly in a position to organize themselves, representatives of the French Jewish community participated in preparing the restitution laws. The Department of Justice tried to modify the restitution rules in favour of the current owners of looted property, but finally lost the battle.[20]

The Decree of April 1945 contained a principled response to spoliation: section 1 stated that the judge was obliged to acknowledge the nullity of any transaction of property performed after the original owner had lost his right to dispose of it. This meant that all transactions performed by so-called 'administrators' were null and void and had to be undone. The judge had very little freedom to decide otherwise since all recipients of despoiled property were considered to have acted in bad faith (with exceptions for some special categories). Another important rule was stated in section 11: possible victims of persecution who had sold their property beforehand were presumed to have acted under duress, unless the buyer could prove he had paid a fair price (in that case the burden of proof switched back to the former owner). There were some exceptions to these rules. Section 1 did not apply to shares and bonds sold on the Paris Stock Exchange.[21] This protection for

---

19 Ibid., p. 98: 'Il faut enfin, prendre des mesures mettant à néant les spoliations voulues par l'ennemi ou inspirées par lui dont beaucoup de citoyens français ont été les victimes. Qu'il s'agisse d'Israélites, de patriotes, -gaullistes ou autres- victimes de condamnations iniques, qu'il s'agisse des Alsaciens ou des Lorraines qui ont été chassés de leur terre paternelle, aucun d'eux ne pourra supporter, de retour en France libérée, de ne pas être réintégré immédiatement dans sa ferme ou son fonds de commerce.' (Translation by the author.)
20 See Mission d'étude sur la spoliation des Juifs de France (Mission-Mattéoli), *Aryanisation économique et restitutions* (Paris 2000), pp. 67-69.
21 See section 13.

the stock market was, as in the Dutch case, motivated by political and economic reasons. I cannot expand on this here, but there are some compelling reasons why, from the perspective of the former owners, the consequences of this exception were less dramatic in the French case than in the Dutch situation.[22] In addition, section 11 did not apply to various kinds of property.

As in the Dutch restitution system, the French legal procedure was speeded up, this time by a fast-track procedure in normal courts. Contrary to the Dutch system, appeal and cassation were permitted, but these did not slow down the process: the executive orders of presiding magistrates were enforceable by anticipation.

Restitution in France and the Netherlands: concluding remarks

In France, the post-war restitution of property rights became an integrated, almost normal part of daily legal life, while in the Netherlands the restitution process remained outside the normal legal system. It became an exceptional, almost exotic legal chapter in the history of Dutch law.

In France, the strict restitution rules made it relatively easy for former owners to get their property back. In addition to this, on the initiative of a French resistance fighter, Professor Émile Terroine, the administration established a Service of Restitutions. This probably unique institution had no judicial powers, but put much effort into verifying whether former Jewish owners were getting their property back.[23] In the Netherlands, on the other hand, Jewish former owners received no support from the Dutch State. They had to fight a harsh, uncertain legal struggle for every item of property they had lost. If the current owner had acquired it in good faith, restitution did not take place. In that case, the former owner had a right to compensation from the assets of the German 'looting institutions' such as Liro that had confiscated the property and sold it during the war. This meant that the amount of compensation was dependent on the total amount of assets these 'looting institutions' possessed at the time of the liberation.[24] After the war, the 'looting institutions' came under the administration of the Dutch State. Liquidation of these institutions took many years. In the late 1940s it became clear from a number of money transactions between Liro and the

---

22 See Mission d'étude sur la spoliation des Juifs de France (Mission-Mattéoli), *La spoliation financière. Volume 1* (Paris 2000), pp. 79-80.
23 See Mission-Mattéoli, *Aryanisation économique et restitutions*, pp. 65-67; 77-83.
24 See Committee on the Investigation of WW II Assets (Scholten-Commission), '*Preface, conclusions and policy recommendations*, (December 1999), pp. 6-7. This English summary and final conclusions from the Dutch Scholten-Commission are available at www.minfin.nl (the site of the Dutch Ministry of Finance). This site contains lots of reports and summaries of Dutch historical commissions of inquiry with regard to spoliation and restitution.

Dutch Central Bank that the latter had greatly profited from Liro assets during the occupation at the expense of dispossessed Jews. Finance Minister Lieftinck refused to pay compensation (dozens of millions Dutch guilders), and an enormous legal battle broke out. This legal battle started in early 1950 and was finally won in August 1952 by a Jewish committee, established by a Jewish lawyer, Heiman Sanders, a born fighter with high principles and many exceptional talents. He was also Lieftinck's chief opponent in the important fields of life insurance policies and securities. Sanders only confided in the Judicial Division and distrusted the other divisions of the Council of Restoration, as well as the Dutch State. His militant, uncompromising attitude anguished his Jewish colleagues, who refused to believe in his lonely struggle.[25]

Nevertheless, Sanders was heard by the Judicial Division of the Council of Restoration and supported by a number of highly reputed Dutch professors of law. His legal struggle could not be a *Blitzkrieg*, as he once said,[26] but it was still extremely successful. The fact that the final material results of the Dutch restitution process for financial assets was ultimately not so bad after all – most people who did not receive restitution of financial assets received compensation of 90%[27] in the early 1950s[28] – is largely thanks to the strength and courage of this one man.

In one of his reports the Director of the French Service of Restitutions, Terroine, once defined restitution as follows:

"a labour both of justice and humanity, which moral and political meaning far transcends the material values in question."[29]

---

25 See Veraart, 'Sanders contra Lieftinck', pp. 193-195.
26 Heiman Sanders, 'Afkoopbare polissen. De eerste bres', in: *Nieuw Israelietisch Weekblad* (Amsterdam, June 19, 1946).
27 In the case of Dutch securities, the final 90% compensation was based on a much more profitable calculation than the one used before: that is why the original Jewish owners of securities felt satisfied with this compensation in the early 1950s. However, the stock exchange contributed almost nothing to this compensation, which was largely paid by the State. The remaining 10% has become subject of recent negotiations between Dutch Jewish organizations and the Amsterdam Stock Exchange. In 2000, the Stock Exchange agreed to pay a substantial amount of money to the Dutch Jewish community.
28 See Committee on the Investigation of WW II Assets (Scholten-Commission), '*Preface, conclusions and policy recommendations*, p. 7. For a general (though not very balanced) overview of the Dutch restitution process and its results, see Gerard Aalders, *Berooid. De beroofde joden en het Nederlandse restitutiebeleid sinds 1945* (Amsterdam 2001).
29 'Pour moi, la restitution des biens spolié aux israélites est une oeuvre à la fois de justice et d'humanité dont la signification morale et politique dépasse de beaucoup les valeurs matérielles en cause.' Émile Terroine, report d.d. December 29, 1944, as cited in Mission d'étude sur la spoliation des Juifs de France (Mission-Mattéoli), *Rapport général* (Paris 2000), p. 13. (Translation by the Mission-Mattéoli.)

It was due to different circumstances, including the establishment of democratic institutions, the presence of strong personalities such as Cassin and Terroine within the De Gaulle administration and last but not least the fact that a relatively large part of the French Jewish community survived the war, that this idea guided the French restitution process from its preparatory phase onwards. It resulted in the Decree of April 1945, which was primarily based on the principle that spoliated owners should be returned to their former situation, irrespective of the good or bad faith of buyers or current owners. This strict principle was closely related to the project of re-establishing a situation of legality, in which 'equality before the law' of all parts of the population was one of the most fundamental principles.

The Dutch administration did not see the restitution process in the same way. As I pointed out before, the Dutch government mainly saw it as one of the exceptional policies necessary for the restoration of the legal system and the economic reconstruction of the country. According to the Minister of Finance, this meant that the restitution process could be blocked or even terminated if it conflicted with other vital economic interests or the financial interests of the Dutch State. Opposing the vision of Lieftinck, Sanders defended his own vision before the Judicial Division of the Council of Restoration. According to Sanders, restitution involved much more than mere material values. In his opinion, it was directly related to the highest values of the Dutch people as a whole. In 1951, in one of his very long pleas before the Judicial Division, he associated the impoverishment of the Netherlands:

> "not only with material deterioration, which had been the fate of the Dutch population since the German invasion. But I also think about the loss of the higher values of our people, the weakening of the apparently unshakeable civil rights, such as the equality of all before the law and the other principles of our constitutional law, most prominently the principle of the independency of the judge, and the respect owed to the principles of the civil law, which the judge cannot put aside while looking up to someone.
> [...]
>
> If you want to consider the struggle I have fought for more than six years for the protection of our [Jewish] community against discrimination and other injustice which have come to us from the east, not as a struggle for material property, but as a struggle against the impoverishment of the Netherlands in the aforementioned sense, this in itself would satisfy me."[30]

---

30 '[Bij de verarming van het vaderland] denk ik niet alleen aan de stoffelijke achteruitgang, welke het lot van het Nederlandse volk is geworden sinds de inval der horden. Maar dan denk ik aan het inboeten van de hogere waarden van ons volk, de verzwakking van de axiomatisch veilig gewaande grondrechten, waaronder de gelijkheid van allen voor de wet en de overige beginselen van ons Staatsrecht, op een der eerste plaatsen het beginsel van de onafhankelijkheid des Rechters, mitsgaders de eerbied voor het

It is clear that Sanders' vision of the post-war restitution of rights corresponded to the dominant vision in France on the restitution process. However, Sanders was the only person in the Netherlands to defend this vision in the immediate post-war years. Sanders did not receive the Noble Prize, as Cassin did in 1968 for his work on human rights. Yet in 1954, a few years before he died, he was decorated by the Dutch State. Sanders was very pleased by this belated national recognition for his work, which had essentially been a struggle against the Dutch State.[31]

Discussion

One cannot make a fair comparison between the restitution policies in France and those in the Netherlands without taking into account three major political, economic and historical differences. Firstly, on a political level, De Gaulle's French National Committee expressed several times during the war that it was deeply motivated to *undo*, as much as possible, the crimes and injustices committed by Vichy. This explains the principled approach of De Gaulle's provisionary parliament and the other legislative organs with regard to the annulment of the spoliations. In the occupied Netherlands, on the other hand, no Vichy had existed. During the German occupation the remaining Dutch civil authorities were civil servants, not politicians. The Dutch government-in-exile refused to accept Dutch State responsibility for crimes committed under German occupation. According to the Dutch government the Germans were entirely responsible for the spoliation and deportation of Dutch Jews, despite evidence of Dutch collaboration.

Secondly, one should keep in mind that immediately after the war the French economy was still virtually intact, while the Dutch economy had been devastated. Thirdly, it is important to note that the liberation of France took place in August - September 1944, while in the northern part of the Netherlands (including Amsterdam) the worst part of the war, the terrible winter of starvation (*hongerwinter*) of 1944-1945, had still to come. By the time the north of the Netherlands had been liberated on 5 May 1945, the inhabitants of this part of the country were completely demoralized. These major political, economic and historical differences should not be ignored

---

privaatrecht, welks grondslagen de Rechter niet op zij mag zetten uit aanzien voor, ja opzien tot een persoon. [...] Indien Gij de strijd welke ik sinds 6 jaren heb gevoerd voor de bescherming van onze volksgroep tegen discriminatie en ander onrecht uit het oosten over ons gekomen, wilt beschouwen, niet als een strijd om materieel bezit, maar als een strijd tegen de verarming van Nederland in de zo-even bedoelde zin, dan zal mij dit op zich zelf reeds tot voldoening strekken.' Plea by Heiman Sanders on 13 November 1951, as cited in Veraart, *Sanders contra Lieftinck*, pp. 198-199. (Translation by the author.)

31 See Martin Levie, 'Mr. Heiman Sanders. Rusteloos strijder voor het recht', in: *Nieuw Israelietisch Weekblad* (Amsterdam, 20 June 1958).

when assessing the differences in vision behind the post-war restitution processes in France and the Netherlands. They explain to a large degree why the Dutch Minister of Finance Lieftinck (1945-1952) was almost entirely focused on the economic reconstruction of the country. However, these factors do not *justify* the fact that the Minister of Finance had so much control over the Dutch restitution process, *nor* the fact that he used this position to block or even end the restitution of despoiled property to the original owners.

The Restitution of 'Aryanized' Property
Recent developments in Austrian Law

Georg GRAF (Salzburg)

I. Introduction

The purpose of this chapter is to give an overview of some interesting recent developments in Austrian Law with respect to property that was taken away under or by the Nazi regime and has not since been returned to its original owners or their heirs. I will refer to such property as 'Aryanized' property, which is a bit of simplification as it was not only Jews who were persecuted and dispossessed by the Nazis.

II. What happened after the German occupation of Austria?

In order to understand these recent developments we need to take a look at what happened in the past. Austria was invaded by German forces on 12 March 1938. This had terrible consequences not only, albeit primarily, for the Jewish population of Austria. These consequences included the systematic taking away of Jewish property.[1]

This happened in two stages. The first wave of dispossession, which started immediately after the German invasion, involved large-scale looting of Jewish homes and businesses. Thousands of self-styled *Kommissars* took possession of Jewish-owned businesses and their contents. The Nazi

---

[1] For a brief overview see H. Witek, '"Arisierungen" in Wien - Aspekte national-sozialistischer Enteignungspolitik 1938–1940', in: Em. Talos et al. (eds.), *NS-Herrschaft in Österreich* (Wien 2000), p. 795 ff. For detailed information see the different publications of the Austrian Historical Commission (*Veröffentlichungen der Österreichischen Historikerkommission. Vermögensentzug während der NS-Zeit sowie Rückstellungen und Entschädigungen seit 1945 in Österreich*, Wien-München, different volumes). Of special relevance to the problem of 'Aryanization' are the following volumes: U. Felber et al., *Ökonomie der Arisierung. Teil 1: Grundzüge, Akteure und Institutionen. Zwangsverkauf, Liquidierung und Restitution von Unternehmen in Österreich 1938 bis 1960; Teil 2: Wirtschaftssektoren, Branchen, Falldarstellungen. Zwangsverkauf, Liquidierung und Restitution von Unternehmen in Österreich 1938 bis 1960* (Wien-München 2004); G. Anderl et al., *"Arisierung" von Mobilien*, (Wien-München 2004); G. Anderl & D. Rupnow, *Die Zentralstelle für jüdische Auswanderung als Beraubungsinstitution*, (Wien-München 2004); Th. Venus & A.-E. Wenck, *Die Entziehung jüdischen Vermögens im Rahmen der Aktion Gildemeester - Eine empirische Studie über Organisation, Form und Wandel von "Arisierung" und jüdischer Auswanderung in Österreich 1938-1941* (Wien-München 2004).

authorities estimated that, in Vienna alone, 7000 such businesses out of a total of 33,000 were dissolved in this process.

The size of these appropriations worried the Nazi authorities, who had other plans for these Jewish assets. Their intention was to make the Jewish businesses available for qualified Aryan purchasers. Therefore certain measures were taken in order to achieve this aim.

In short, the Nazis started a systematic approach towards 'Aryanization'. Among other things this required all Jews to register their assets by the end of June 1938 so that the Nazis knew exactly what they could take. A special central organisation (*Vermögensverkehrsstelle*) was set up for the purposes of 'aryanizing' Jewish assets. This was located at the Ministry of Economy and Labour and started work in April 1938. Its work was swiftly completed, with the Nazis looking at all businesses they qualified as Jewish and deciding in each case whether the business should be closed down or should survive under Aryan control. In the case of larger enterprises, official administrators were appointed to find qualified buyers.

The sums paid by the buyers were deposited on special bank accounts; most of the money was appropriated by the Nazis, who made Jews pay special taxes such as the *Reichsfluchtsteuer* or *Judenvermögensabgabe*. In general the purchase prices paid by buyers were low, reflecting the decreased value of Jewish businesses for their owners. In the hands of Aryan owners, however, they had a much higher value. To avoid windfall gains, Aryan buyers had to pay a special tax ('Aryanization tax'). The Nazi government therefore profited twice from these sales: Firstly it got the money deposited on the special accounts, while secondly it got the Aryanization tax.

On 1 February 1939 the *Vermögensverkehrsstelle* noted that three quarters of Jewish businesses listed for survival had already been 'aryanized'. If we look back at these transactions, we can see that most of them took place under the guise of normal legal transactions. That appearance, of course, was deceptive as in most cases there was no free consent of the parties. Jews simply had to give away their property in order to be allowed to leave the country. Not only did they have to sell their businesses, but also all their other assets, including works of art, jewellery, houses and anything else they may have owned.

Not all Jews, however, were able to leave the country under this scheme. Those who remained were deported to concentration camps and their property was also taken away. In the case of these victims, the Nazis did not generally go to the trouble of disguising the thefts as legal transactions. People deported to concentration camps were simply ordered to hand over their property to the German State. For those who managed to keep some assets it was ordered that, after their death, everything would go to the German State.

III. Austrian Restitution Laws after 1945

After the war it took quite some time for the government of the liberated Austria to realize that it had to do something to enable restitution of this stolen property. Ultimately, however, the Austrian Parliament passed a number of laws for this purpose.[2]

The very first of these was what is referred to as the 'Annulment Act' [*Nichtigkeitsgesetz*],[3] which declared all transactions and other legal acts carried out during the financial or political penetration of Austria by the German Reich and resulting in the confiscation of property or property rights with or without payment of compensation to be null and void. The Annulment Act was only of a declaratory nature. The granting of restitution rights to owners who had suffered losses was expressly reserved for subsequent legislation. Therefore, the Annulment Act did not have any practical effect; in that respect it was a rather strange law.

Between 1946 and 1949 seven restitution acts were passed. These applied not only to 'Aryanized' property, but in general to property that had been taken away on political grounds during the German occupation of Austria. Not only Jews, but also other victims of the Nazi regime – such as political opponents or the Catholic Church – were able to demand restitution of their assets under these acts.

The First Restitution Act[4] was enacted in 1946; it dealt with property that had been taken away by the German State itself and was now in the possession of the Austrian State. The Second Restitution Act[5] applied to property that the Austrian State had confiscated from people who were war criminals or members of a Nazi organisation.

The Third Restitution Act, which was enacted in 1947,[6] was the most important restitution legislation as it applied generally to property wrongfully taken away from its owners and transferred to private individuals or businesses.

These three acts were accompanied by four other restitution acts dealing with specific aspects of the problem. The Fourth Restitution Act[7] provided for the reinstatement of company names that had been changed under

---

2   For a comprehensive overview see G. Graf, *Die österreichische Rückstellungsgesetzgebung. Eine juristische Analyse* (Wien München 2003); B. Bailer-Galanda, *Die Entstehung der Rückstellungs- und Entschädigungsgesetzgebung: Die Republik Österreich und das in der NS-Zeit entzogene Vermögen* (Wien-München 2003).
3   BGBl 1946/106. ('BGBl' stands for *Bundesgesetzblatt*, the Federal Law Gazette).
4   BGBl 1946/156.
5   BGBl 1947/53.
6   BGBl 1947/54.
7   BGBl 1947/143.

National Socialist coercion. The Fifth Restitution Act[8] concerned the restitution of the rights and interests of shareholders or partners in businesses where the entity in which they had had an ownership interest had been 'Aryanized' and had subsequently ceased to exist. The Sixth Restitution Act[9] dealt with the restitution of confiscated patents, trade name and pattern rights. The Seventh Restitution Act[10] concerned the restitution of employee rights, such as claims for wages, severance payments and pensions. Special courts ('Restitution Commissions') were set up to adjudicate claims arising from the restitution acts. There were three instances, the highest of which was the Supreme Restitution Commission and consisted of Austrian Supreme Court judges.

These seven restitution acts tried to cover most aspects of the problem of property wrongfully taken away during the Nazi occupation of Austria. There was, however, one aspect of the problem for which the government completely failed to provide a solution. This was the problem of tenancy agreements. During the German occupation more than 200,000 Jewish tenants had to leave their homes. New tenants soon moved in. After the liberation of Austria the government failed to enact restitution legislation with respect to the rights of these former tenants. The political pressure against such legislation was too strong, with the pressure coming mainly from those people who had moved into 'Aryanized' apartments. Those who were deprived of their rights as tenants during the occupation have never received compensation.

One of the reasons for this failure by the Austrian Government was the victim thesis, to which the government subscribed. According to this thesis, Austria had been the first victim of Nazi Germany. Therefore – according to the official position – Austria was not responsible for crimes committed during the German occupation and so could not be held liable for the damage inflicted on the victims of Nazi terror. This victim thesis was, of course, highly problematic as many Austrians had actively participated in the Nazi crimes.

The failure to resolve the problem of tenancy agreements was an immediate consequence of the victim thesis. This becomes obvious if one takes into consideration that it would have been very problematic to evict all the new tenants, many of whom had not been personally involved in the original 'Aryanization'. The whole matter was, therefore, a complex problem requiring a complex solution. Any possible solution would by necessity have included an element of compensation. If the government had allowed the former tenants to return to their apartments, it would have had to com-

---

8 BGBl 1949/164.
9 BGBl 1949/199.
10 BGBl 1949/207.

pensate those who now had to move out, whereas opting for a different solution would have meant making payments to the former tenants. The unwillingness of the Austrian Government to make any payments made it impossible to resolve this problem.

In addition to the seven restitution acts the Austrian Government enacted a number of other laws to deal with the problem of assets wrongfully taken away during the Nazi occupation and for which no restitution claims had been filed. As restitution claims were inheritable only to a certain extent and as there were many cases where the former owners had died without any heirs, there were a lot of such unclaimed assets. It took the Austrian State more than fifteen years, however, to find a solution for this problem.

This solution consisted in the creation of two collection points[11] that were entitled to file claims for the restitution of property wrongfully taken away and which had not yet been returned to the former owners. There were two collection points, one for the Jewish victims of Nazism and one for other victims. The collection points were legal entities, which had to assert restitution claims for those objects that had not yet been restituted. The assets that they successfully claimed were used to pay compensation to victims of Nazism, with 80% of the proceeds of the restituted assets going to Jewish victims and 20% to other victims.[12] Whether these percentages adequately reflected the proportions of damage suffered by these two groups of Nazi victims is debated.

The result of the restitution process was that restitution took place to a certain extent, but there were also many cases where there was no restitution or no satisfactory restitution. There are many different reasons for these failures. Firstly, there were shortcomings in the legislation itself. Art works, for example, that were sold at public auctions did not have to be restituted, providing the purchaser had acted in good faith.[13] In many cases, the restitution commissions found that buyers had indeed acted in good faith. Secondly, there was no public support for the victims of 'Aryanization'. People who owned 'Aryanized' property did not generally return it voluntarily; for each asset it was necessary to initiate legal proceedings, which could be expensive and risky.

IV. New developments

Although restitution had quite substantial shortcomings, the official version was, of course, different. According to this version, Austria had done

---

11 Referred to as *Sammelstellen*; cf. *Auffangorganisationengesetz*, BGBl 1957/73.
12 Cf BGBl 1962/108.
13 Cf § 4 of the Third Restitution Act.

everything it could do to return 'Aryanized' property to its former owners. In the 1990s, however, public opinion changed. For the first time Austrian politicians acknowledged the active participation of Austrians in the Holocaust. This change in public opinion alone, however, would not have been enough to 'reopen the restitution files'. For this, a certain amount of outside pressure was necessary. It all started when the authorities in New York seized a painting by Schiele because the heirs of its original owner claimed that it had been 'Aryanized'.

This seizure prompted the Austrian government to appoint a commission to search through the collections of state-owned museums for 'Aryanized' property. The commission found a lot of art works that had not been restituted after the Second World War. In response to the commission's findings the Austrian Parliament enacted legislation to restitute art works owned by the State.[14]

In 1999 a commission of historians was established to "research and report about the whole complex of looting of property in the territory of the Republic of Austria in the Nazi era and acts of restitution and/or compensation (including economic and social benefits) by the Republic of Austria after 1945." This commission worked for the next four years and published 49 volumes of research results; thanks to its work we now have a much broader and clearer picture of what happened both during and after the Nazi regime with respect to stolen property.

In 2000 a change of government took place. The Conservatives formed a coalition with the Freedom Party of Jörg Haider. This new government was not welcomed with much enthusiasm in Europe; indeed the rest of Europe tried to isolate it. Another problem the government had to deal with was the class actions brought in the United States against Austria and Austrian enterprises by victims of 'Aryanization' and slave labour. At first the new government took a defensive position, but then it started talks with all relevant groups and these resulted in an agreement with the United States.[15]

This agreement led to three important acts:

The first was the Reconciliation Fund Act,[16] which sought to make payments available to former slave labourers. Quite a respectable amount of money was put into a special fund and former slave labourers could get up to 7630 euros each. This fund subsequently made payments totalling 352 million euros to 131,000 people.[17]

---

14 Bundesgesetz vom 4. Dezember 1998 über die Rückgabe von Kunstgegenständen aus den Österreichischen Bundesmuseen und Sammlungen; BGBl I 1998/181.
15 Published in BGBl III 2001/121.
16 Versöhnungsfondsgesetz, BGBl I 2000/74.
17 Details can be found on the homepage of the Fund: www.versoehnungsfonds.at.

The second act[18] provided compensation for tenancy agreements. As we have seen above, one of the main shortcomings of Austrian restitution legislation was that it did not provide compensation for lost tenancies. One of the first reports of the Historical Commission[19] dealt with this matter in detail. The new legislation provides compensation for these leases, as well as for household property and personal valuables and effects. Each applicant will be awarded 7,000 dollars, but a further 1,000 dollars per person may also be paid out.

The third act was the General Settlement Fund Law,[20] the first part of which provides financial compensation for stolen property that has not been restituted. A fund totalling 210 million dollars has been set up for this purpose.

Those eligible to file an application are persons "who were persecuted by the National Socialist regime on political grounds, on grounds of origin, religion, nationality, sexual orientation, or of physical or mental handicap or of accusations of so-called anti-sociality, or who left the country to escape such persecution, and who suffered loss or damage as a result of or in connection with events having occurred on the territory of the present-day Republic of Austria during the National Socialist era." Compensation is paid for five different categories of assets: a) liquidated businesses, including licences and other business assets; b) real estate, unless in *rem* restitution pursuant to the second part of this act has been granted; c) bank accounts, stocks, bonds, mortgages; d) movable property, unless such property losses are covered by the Amendment to the Federal Law to establish the National Fund of the Republic of Austria for Victims of National Socialism (Federal Law Gazette I No. 11/2001), and e) insurance policies.

This legislation was enacted in January 2001; unfortunately it took more than five years for the fund to make its first payments. The reason for this was a clause stating that payments could be made only after all claims in the United States pending as of 30 June 2001 against Austria or Austrian companies arising out of or related to the National Socialist era or World War II had been dismissed. That moment was reached on 7 December 2005.

In the meantime the financial resources available to the fund have proven to be insufficient. Each applicant will only get compensation in the amount of about 10% of his original claim. This is quite frustrating as it shows the extent to which people suffered losses during the Nazi regime for which they have not received compensation.

---

18 BGBl I 2001/11.
19 Österreichische Historikerkommission (ed.), *"Arisierung" und Rückstellung von Wohnungen in Wien* (Wien-München 2004).
20 BGBl I 2001/12.

The second part of the legislation is more interesting than the first part from a legal point of view. It concerns not only compensation, but also restitution. It provides for in *rem* restitution of publicly owned property. If real estate was 'Aryanized' and has not been restituted, it can be reclaimed, provided it is publicly owned. That condition is fulfilled if it is owned by the State or a company that is itself 100% owned by the State. The legislation does not, however, cover real estate owned by private entities.

Claims for in *rem* restitution are decided by an arbitration panel consisting of three members: one nominated by Austria, one by the United States and the third, the chairman, by the other two members. Although the panel makes only recommendations, these are followed by the government.

The panel can make recommendations only with respect to property that was never the subject of a claim previously ruled on by an Austrian court or administrative body or settled by agreement and for which the claimant or a relative has never otherwise received compensation or other consideration. However, there is one important exception to this rule: even in such cases the panel can make a positive recommendation if it unanimously determines that a previous decision or settlement constituted an extreme injustice.

What is the reason for this exemption? During the negotiations with the victims' lawyers and the United States Austria maintained that the new legislation should not apply to cases that had already been decided or settled in another way. This, however, was not acceptable to the other side, and so this interesting compromise was reached.

Obviously the Austrians thought that there would not be so many cases on which a decision had previously been taken. That assumption turned out to be wrong. The arbitration panel has received a lot of applications on which there had been a settlement or court decision in the past. So far the panel has ruled on only a small number of cases, but in some of these it found the previous settlement or decision to be extremely unjust and therefore recommended restitution of the property.[21]

For a lawyer the concept of extreme injustice[22] is extremely interesting. Most lawyers are happy that in general they do not have to find out what is

---

21 All decisions of the arbitration panel are published on the homepage of the Nationalfonds: www.nationalfonds.org.
22 See Graf, '"Arisierung" und Restitution, Anmerkungen zum Entschädigungsfondsgesetz', *Juristische Blätter (JBl)* (2001), pp. 746-755; Franz-Stefan Meissel, 'Unrechtsbewältigung durch Rechtsgeschichte? Zum Begriff der "extremen Ungerechtigkeit" im Entschädigungsfondsgesetz', *Juridikum* 1 (2003), pp. 42-46; W.H. Rechberger, 'Ist Ungerechtigkeit komparationsfähig? Zum Begriff der "extremen Ungerechtigkeit" in § 10 Entschädigungsfondsgesetz', *Juridikum* (2005), p. 59. The views of the arbitration panel are defended in a paper by two law clerks of the panel: F. Azizi & G. Gößler, 'Extreme Ungerechtigkeit und bewegliches System', *Juristische Blätter (JBl)* 7 (2006), pp. 415-436.

just, but only what is in accordance with the law. Justice is a criterion primarily addressed by the lawmaker, but not the lawyer. The General Settlement Fund Law, however, forces arbitrators to reflect on the concept of justice and its opposite, the concept of injustice. And that is not all: it is not injustice, but rather extreme injustice that the arbitration panel has to concern itself with. What makes this task even more difficult is the fact that the law itself is completely silent about what should count as extreme injustice.

V. Problems of the concept of extreme injustice

In the remainder of this chapter I will take a critical look at what the arbitration panel has to say about extreme injustice. The panel has developed an interesting concept[23] of what it takes for a past decision to be extremely unjust. This concept is unfortunately not without problems.

This concept has three elements. The first element refers to the outcome of the decision. According to the panel a decision can only be extremely unjust if there is a substantial difference between the actual outcome of the decision and the outcome that would have been achieved if the restitution legislation had been applied correctly. That is obviously correct. If the law is concerned only with extreme injustice, there must be a substantial difference between the correct and actual outcomes of the case. Unfortunately the panel refuses to specify precise criteria on how significant the difference must be in order for the prior decision to be considered extremely unjust. That, of course, is not accidental, but intentional, as the panel does not want to bind itself.

According to the panel, this difference between the actual and correct outcomes of the case is only a necessary and not a sufficient condition for extreme injustice. The panel maintains that in order to qualify as extreme injustice the earlier decision must fulfil a second condition. And here the panel makes a distinction between cases where there has been a previous court decision and those where there has been a private settlement between the parties.

A court decision can be extremely unjust only if the decision was based on an "objectively indefensible application of the relevant legal norms." What does that mean? It means obviously that the court must have arrived at its decision through seriously defective legal reasoning. If a decision was defensible, no extreme injustice could have existed.

In cases where there was a settlement, a different condition must be fulfilled. A settlement – the panel claims – can be extremely unjust only if there was inequality of bargaining power between the parties who made the agreement. This can be the case if the 'decision freedom' of a party was

---

23 See, for example, the decisions 3/2003, 27/2005, 64/2006, 88/2006, 204/2006.

restricted or if a party did not have all the information that was necessary to make a well-informed decision.

Let me give a very instructive example of how the panel applies this criterion. This is the case of the palace[24] belonging to the Jewish Bloch-Bauer family. Ferdinand Bloch-Bauer was one of the richest men in Austria before the National Socialist occupation. His family held shares in a big sugar company, of which he was the president. He had a spectacular art collection, including a number of paintings by Klimt.[25] The family also owned an impressive palace in the first district of Vienna. The Nazis were highly interested in these assets. What did they do? They sent the tax inspectors to the sugar company, and those tax inspectors – unsurprisingly – stated that the company, and specifically its president, had failed to pay enormous amounts of taxes.[26] In reality these debts in all probability did not exist. In order to pay these taxes Bloch-Bauer had to sell all his property, and even that was not enough to pay all the taxes. Bloch-Bauer himself was able to flee before the Nazi authorities could arrest him.

After the end of the Nazi regime the family tried to get back its property, which was now in the possession of the State. This proved to be difficult because the State did not want to return these assets. The State's representatives argued that this had not been an 'Aryanization' because Bloch-Bauer had had to pay his taxes just like any other citizen. That, of course, was not a very promising line of argument. Therefore another strategy was chosen. The State realized that the shares in the sugar company formed the most valuable part of the Bloch-Bauer assets. In order to get the shares back soon – so it was speculated – the family would be willing to give up the palace. The State lawyers consequently threatened to delay restitution of the shares unless the family was willing to give up the palace. And that is what happened: a settlement was reached in which the family got back the sugar company shares in return for giving up its claim to the palace and payment of 1.5 million Schillings.

The arbitration panel found this settlement to be extremely unjust. Both elements of extreme injustice that the panel deemed to be essential were realized with respect to this settlement. Firstly there was a big difference

---

24 Case 88/2006.
25 After a long legal struggle, five very valuable pictures by Klimt were returned to the heirs of Ferdinand Bloch-Bauer in 2006. Some of the legal aspects of this case are discussed in G. Graf, 'Überlegungen zum Anwendungsbereich des § 1 Z 2 KunstrückgabeG', *Österreichische Notariats Zeitung (NZ)* (2005), p. 321. For more information about the restitution claims of the family, see www.adele.at. See also the decision of the Claims Resolution Tribunal http://www.crt-ii.org/_awards/_apdfs Osterreichische _Zuckerindustrie.pdf.
26 Cf R. Faber & F.-S. Meissel, *Nationalsozialistisches Steuerrecht und Restitution* (Wien 2006).

between the actual and correct outcomes of the restitution proceedings. Furthermore – and this is the second element – the decision freedom of the family was restricted. As they had to get the shares back in order to gain control over the company, their bargaining position was weakened; a fact that was exploited by the State. In this case the panel obviously reached a sound decision.

This does not, however, mean that the conceptual framework within which the panel operates is without problems. The main problem is that the panel is too strict with regard to what constitutes a restriction of decision freedom. The panel qualifies a settlement as extremely unjust only if there is proof of a specific restriction on the claimants' decision freedom. If there are no indications of such a specific restriction, the settlement cannot be considered extremely unjust even if the claimants received only a very small compensation payment.

Let me give an example. In 2006[27] the panel had to decide on a case where the value of the property was at least 60,000, but probably closer to 180,000 Schillings. That was in any event the price for which the property was sold three years later. Under the settlement, the original owners gave up their claim in exchange for compensation of 6,000 Schillings. They therefore received no more than 10% of the value of the property, and maybe as little as 3%. Nevertheless the panel did not qualify the settlement as extremely unjust. It could not find any specific indications that the claimants' decision freedom had been restricted and so claimed that they had made a free and fully informed decision, thus exercising their private autonomy. Private autonomy – the panel argued – gives you the right to make contracts that are disadvantageous to you; therefore even a very disadvantageous settlement can be valid.

The panel's remarks with respect to private autonomy as a general concept are perfectly true; the way in which the panel applies this concept with respect to such settlements is, however, very much open to dispute. What the panel fails to do is to ask why the claimants had accepted such a disadvantageous settlement. There is only one answer to this question: the claimants were not in a position to risk continuing the lawsuit. They were in such a weak position that it was rational for them to accept ridiculously low compensation. And this answer is confirmed by what historians tell us. Nazi victims and their heirs were in weak psychological and financial positions. Settlements made by them were not generally made from a position of strength, but weakness.

This is a very important fact that has to be taken into consideration when applying the concept of extreme injustice to such settlements. Given this structural disadvantage of the typical claimant in a restitution lawsuit, it

---

27 Case 46/2006. The panel has since overturned the original decision, cf CA WA 2/2007.

should not be necessary to demand proof of any additional restriction of the claimant's decision freedom in order for the settlement to be qualified as extremely unjust, providing the settlement was such that the original owner received compensation that was not in proportion to the value of the property in question. Such a settlement is in itself an irrefutable indication that it was made under conditions in which one party was in a significantly weaker position. This should be enough to qualify such a settlement as extremely unjust.

VI. Final remark

One final point: The laws presented in this paper are obviously important insofar as they provide either compensation or restitution in cases where there had been no restitution or compensation in the past. In the long run, however, the real importance of these laws will turn out to be different. Their real importance will be historical rather than legal. These laws received very broad publicity. Thousands of people made applications for compensation, while fewer applied for restitution. In these applications each applicant tells a story of persecution and theft, either their own story or that of their parents, grandparents or other relatives. Taken together these applications give us a very detailed picture not only of events taking place during the Nazi occupation of Austria, but also of what happened after the Second World War to those who wanted their property back or at least some compensation for the loss of their property. These applications give us a very dramatic picture of how difficult it was to get back one's property. They also show that it was often impossible to get back stolen property and that people often had to settle for ridiculously low compensation. Taken together these thousands of applications contain information that will be invaluable for future historians. So even if these recent laws do not provide for adequate compensation, they will at least provide plenty of information for future historians.

The Restitution of the Munch Painting *Summer Night on the Beach* under the Austrian Art Restitution Act 1998

Franz-Stefan MEISSEL (Vienna)

Introduction

The following chapter deals with the legal questions concerning the restitution of the Munch painting *Summer Night on the Beach*, which was formerly owned by Alma Mahler-Werfel and until recently could be admired by the public in the prestigious state-owned Austrian Gallery of the Belvedere in Vienna. Specific attention is paid to the provisions of the Austrian Art Restitution Act [*KunstrückgabeG*] 1998. This Federal Statute on the Restitution of Art Objects from Austrian Federal museums and collections (BGBl I No. 181/1998) was supposed to form the legal basis for the "fast and unbureaucratic restitution of unjustifiably acquired art objects to their owners or their legal successors"[1] who had been the object of persecution during the Nazi period.

The term 'unjustifiably acquired' in this context should be understood in a moral rather than strictly legal sense. The law authorizes the return of art objects that, in a strictly legal sense, are indisputably owned by the Federal Republic, but have been acquired in ways causing *moral or historical concern*. In other words, in the Art Restitution Act 1998 the Republic of Austria allows for a modified self-conception in restitution matters, according to which the Republic *at least morally accepts a share of the responsibility* for the injustices that occurred during the National Socialist period. This responsibility is also reflected in various new legal provisions ensuring payments to victims of National Socialism. In 1995, for instance, this led to the establishment of the Austrian National Fund in order to "express the special responsibility of Austria vis-à-vis victims of National Socialism" (section 1 *para* 2 National Fund Law [*NationalfondsG*] BGBl 432/1995) and to the express acknowledgement in the General Settlement Fund Law of the "moral responsibility for losses and damage that have been inflicted on the victims of National Socialism as a consequence of or in connection with the National Socialist regime" (section 1 *para* 2 *leg cit*). The provisions of the Art Restitution Act 1998 must be seen in the context of these novel restitution laws aimed at the overall elimination of shortcomings and gaps in restitution laws and restitution practices after 1945.

---

[1] Member of the Austrian Parliament [*Nationalrat*] Andreas Khol in his speech in the debate on the Art Restitution Act on 5 November 1998.

The case of Alma Mahler-Werfel's Munch painting *Summer Night on the Beach* is a prominent example of a quest for restitution of art that had been unsuccessful until 2006. As the story of this case and the legal questions involved are long and rather complicated, this paper is divided into two sections.

The first section presents the circumstances of the case ('The Course of Events') by providing an account of the restitution proceedings and the attempts to reach a settlement by Alma Mahler-Werfel in the immediate post-war era as well as her granddaughter Marina's more recent attempts at restitution and the rejection by the Art Restitution Advisory Board [*Kunstrückgabebeirat*] in 1999 of a recommendation for restitution.

The reasons behind the negative opinion expressed by the Art Restitution Advisory Board in 1999 are analyzed in the second section, with specific examination of the purpose of the Art Restitution Act 1998 and the prerequisites for restitution under section 1 clause 2 *leg cit*. Special attention will be paid to the questionable relevance of the legally binding rejection of the claim by the Upper Restitution Commission of Vienna (URC) [*Rückstellungsoberkommission Wien (ROK)*] in 1953. In this context, apart from a critical analysis of the URC's decision in 1953, attention is also given to the legal evaluations in the question of legally binding, but in particular cases extremely unjust decisions, as since established in the General Settlement Fund Law [*EntschädigungsfondsG*] 2001.

The positive impact of these arguments on the Advisory Board in its final recommendation of 2006 is discussed in the final part of the paper.

Course of Events

The historical background of the case is presented in chronological order below. This requires a distinction between events during the Nazi regime (A.), restitution procedures during the post-war era (B.) and recent attempts towards restitution following the entering into force of the Art Restitution Act 1998 (C.).

The files[2] stored in the Archives of Vienna (*Wiener Stadt- und Landesarchiv*), which also include the files of the pre-proceedings,[3] allow reconstruction of the circumstances under which the Munch painting was sold, as well as the course of the restitution proceedings from the filing of the claim

---

2   Wiener Stadt- und Landesarchiv [Archives of Vienna], Regional State Court for Civil Matters, A 29 Restitution Commission Rk 216/61; the file contains the order numbers 1 – 123 in volume 1 and 124 – 163 in volume 2 and consists of a total of 556 pages.
3   The former file numbers of the proceedings Rk 216/61 are 63 R k 364/47, 63 R k 1372/48, 63 Rk 187/53 and 3 Rk 96/55. The two proceedings before the URC Vienna have file numbers Rkb 1116/48 and Rkb 186/53, the two revision proceedings before the SRC Rkv 219/48 and Rkv 152/53. Order numbers or file numbers cited in the following refer to the omnibus file Rk 216/61.

in 1947 until Alma Mahler-Werfel's death in 1964.[4] The proceedings before the Art Restitution Advisory Board have been traced on the basis of correspondence and documents provided by Marina Mahler.

A. Alma's Family Background

First of all the biographical backgrounds of the people involved will be briefly recapitulated: Alma Mahler-Werfel was the daughter of Jakob Emil Schindler and his wife Anna Bergen. Schindler was a famous landscape painter and is considered by art historians to have been the most important Austrian impressionist painter of his time.

After Schindler's early death, Alma's mother married his pupil Carl Moll. Moll was not only a renowned painter, but also a skilful and influential art dealer. This second marriage of Alma's mother produced another daughter, Marie. Alma's half-sister was married to the judge Dr Richard Eberstaller, a convinced National Socialist, who became Vice President of the Regional State Court for Criminal Matters [*Landesgericht für Strafsachen*] in Vienna. Alma's mother, Anna Bergen-Moll, died in 1938.

Alma was a talented musician and even composed a number of songs herself. In 1901 she married Gustav Mahler, who was then the director of the Royal Opera House in Vienna. After Mahler's death she married Walter Gropius, the architect and founder of the Bauhaus school of design. Her third husband was the bestselling author Franz Werfel. In the 1930s Alma and Franz Werfel openly sympathized with the 'corporatist state' in Austria, an authoritarian regime that oppressed left-wing parties on the one hand and also the pro-German national socialist movement on the other hand.

B. The Munch Painting and Events during the Nazi Regime

The Munch painting *Summer Night on the Beach* was given to Alma in 1916 as a present on the occasion of the birth of her beloved daughter

---

4 The facts of the case have been studied by a number of authors in recent years. See for instance: Hubertus Czernin, 'Gewissenlose Räuber', *Der Standard* (2 April 1999); Hubertus Czernin, 'Einfach nur Pech gehabt', *Der Standard* (17 August 1999); Hubertus Czernin, 'Der Triumph der Bürokratie', *Der Standard* (4 November 1999); Franz-Stefan Meissel, 'Edvard Munchs "Sommernacht am Strand" und das Restitutionsverfahren Alma Mahler-Werfels gegen die Republik Österreich', in: M. Luminati et al. (eds.), *Mit den Augen der Rechtsgeschichte: Rechtsfälle - selbstkritisch kommentiert* (Berlin/ Münster/ Wien/ Zürich/ London 2007); Sophie Lillie, *Was einmal war. Handbuch der enteigneten Kunstsammlungen Wiens* (Wien 2003), p. 735 ff.; Michael Wladika, '"Ersuche ich daher ... in keiner Weise Frau Alma Mahler-Werfel entgegenzukommen"', in: V. Pawlowski & H. Wendelin (eds.), *Enteignete Kunst. Raub und Rückgabe - Österreich von 1938 bis heute* (Wien 2006) p. 79 ff.; Franz-Stefan Meissel & Julia Jungwirth, 'Moralisch verständlich, aber rechtlich nichts zu machen?', in: Pawlowski & Wendelin (eds.), *Enteignete Kunst*, p. 104 ff.

Manon (who died in 1935).[5] Alma later claimed that the Munch painting meant more to her than any other painting. In 1937 Alma gave five paintings on a two-year loan to the Austrian Gallery at the Belvedere,[6] among them *Summer night on the Beach* by Edvard Munch.

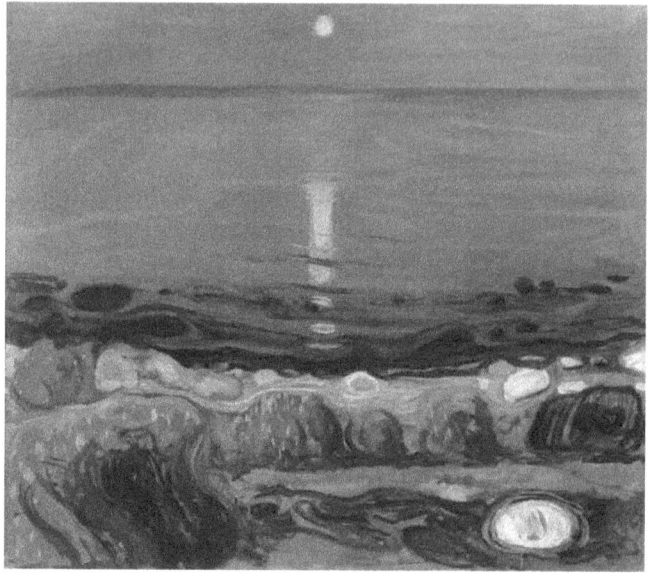

Edvard Munch, Summer Night on the Beach
(Oil on canvas, 103 x 120 cm, Private Collection)

Immediately after the *Anschluss* (the annexation of Austria by the German Reich), Alma hastily left Austria (13 March 1938). Alma Mahler-Werfel's villa at Hohe Warte, Steinfeldgasse 2, a luxurious estate designed by Josef Hoffmann, was confiscated by the Gestapo. The Werfels first went to

---

5   Compare Mahler-Werfel, *Mein Leben* (Frankfurt am Main 1960), p. 82 ff [*translation*]: "Gropius, an incredibly noble person, had the intense wish to make me a grand present after the birth of the child. So he wrote to Karl Reininghaus, who from time to time sold one of the paintings from his ample collection, and asked him to sell the *Midnight Sun* by Edvard Munch. On the same day two servants arrived with the painting and a moving letter from Karl Reininghaus. He wrote that the painting had belonged to me for many years because I loved it so much. Only he had not found the right occasion for sending it to me. I would have obtained it with my smile! Now I could sink into this oily calm and still so vivid sea for days. No painting has ever touched me the way this one has."

6   The other paintings lent to the Gallery were *Rocky Coast near Ragusa, Forest Road near St. Gilgen* and *Forest Path* by Jakob Emil Schindler and a portrait of Alma by Oskar Kokoschka. The acceptance of the paintings was confirmed in a written document of 2 August 1937 by Dr Heinrich Schwarz on behalf of the Austrian Gallery.

France, until they had to flee again; in a strenuous journey they eventually reached New York.

During the Nazi period Professor Carl Moll, together with his daughter and son-in-law, resided at Wollergasse 10,[7] directly opposite Alma's confiscated villa, and temporarily at Villa Mahler in Breitenstein on the Semmering.[8] This villa in the countryside had been given as a gift to her half-sister, Marie Eberstaller, by Alma Mahler-Werfel in June 1939, obviously in order to prevent the villa from being confiscated like Alma's Viennese mansion.

On 18 March 1938 (shortly after the Werfels' escape) Carl Moll, allegedly at Alma's request, achieved the return of the borrowed paintings from the Austrian Gallery (renamed 'Gallery of the 19th Century' during the Nazi period). At the same time he was already negotiating with Professor Bruno Grimschitz, the director of the Gallery, on the sale of the Munch painting. Alma Mahler-Werfel tried to find a buyer in France and was thinking about bringing the painting abroad with the help of a friend working as a diplomat.

Finally the Munch painting was sold in 1940 to the Gallery of the 19th Century by Marie Eberstaller (in her own name) for 7,000 RM. The written confirmation of the sales contract by Professor Grimschitz contains no reference to Alma Mahler-Werfel nor to any authorization from her. Grimschitz, however, according to his own account in the following trials, assumed that the proceeds were to be used to repair the roof of the villa in Breitenstein/Semmering; indeed such a repair was actually carried out.[9] At the end of the war (in the night of 12 - 13 April 1945), Moll and the Eberstallers all committed suicide.[10]

---

7 In the lawsuit Alma Mahler-Werfel *v.* Anton Klement (21 Cg 294/47), among others regarding the right of succession, the Regional State Court for Civil Matters stated: "On the bases of the witness reports of Arch. Willi Legler, Anna Murauer, Therese Görtz and Ida Wagner-Gebauer, as well as Stefan and Katharina Wallner, it has been established that the married couple Eberstaller had various moveable assets [note: namely numerous carpets, silver dishes, paintings] transported from the plaintiff's villa [in Döbling] to the [neighbouring] villa Moll after the plaintiff's departure in 1938, that these were property of the plaintiff and that Dr Eberstaller had disposed of such objects in his last will of 11 April 1945... ." (Judgement of 22 March 1948, p. 89 of the file).
8 EZ 429 Breitenstein cadastral register. For the purpose of a gift Alma Mahler-Werfel, who had fled abroad, gives special authority to the lawyer Dr Otto Hein, who would later represent her in the restitution proceedings.
9 The repair of the roof costed approximately 1,500 RM. Some plumbing was also done in the house (the construction of a wooden fence and the installation of a water closet) for about 400 RM (this was the result of the investigation of the circumstances in the decision 63 Rk 1372/48 = order number 91, p. 4 ff).
10 According to one version Soviet soldiers supposedly entered the house beforehand and wounded Carl Moll when he was attempting to protect his daughter from being raped (according to Menges, Carl Moll, *Neue Deutsche Biographie*, volume 17 (Berlin 1994)

C. Restitution Procedures under the Third Restitution Act

After the defeat of the Nazi Regime, the Austrian Annulment Act of 1946 [*NichtigkeitsG*, BGBL Nr 106/1946] declared all transfers of property to be null and void that had "occurred during the German occupation of Austria in the course of its political and economical penetration by the German Reich." The enforcement of this provision was reserved for subsequent legislation, which followed in the form of seven Restitution Acts in 1946 – 1949. These provided for restitution in kind of property which was "wrongfully withdrawn" ("*entzogen*") from people who were victims of the Nazi regime or in cases in which the transfer of property would not have taken place without the National Socialist takeover.

Alma Mahler-Werfel now tried to recover her assets in Austria. She got back the ownership of her villa in the countryside[11] and also her mansion in Vienna. The tricky part was restitution of the paintings from the Austrian Gallery.

1. First Ruling of the Restitution Commission in 1948

In her restitution claim filed on 14 August 1947 at the Restitution Commission of Vienna (RC Vienna), Alma requested restitution of two paintings: *Summer Night on the Beach* by Edvard Munch and *Rocky Coast near Ragusa* by Jakob Emil Schindler pursuant to the Third Restitution Act 1947. The disputed amount indicated in the restitution claim drafted by the lawyer Dr Otto Hein in Alma's name amounted to 15,000 Austrian Schillings. The Federal Republic of Austria as defendant was represented in the trial by the Federal Law Office [*Finanzprokuratur*].

The proceedings before the RC Vienna chaired by Dr Adolf Ehrenzweig (a well-known expert in private law, who was later promoted to the position of professor at the University of Vienna) ended with the ruling of 24 September 1948 that dismissed the suit owing to the Federal Republic of Austria's lack of capacity as a defendant, given that the property concerned was

---

p. 737). Sure enough the file contains the copy of a letter dated 10 April 1945 by Carl Moll to Drl. Ottmann, the Secretary of the Society of Museum Friends [*Gesellschaft der Museumsfreunde*], in which he announces the suicide beforehand: "We three have decided to go to sleep together and not to wake up again ... My son in law, however, as director, president of the Criminal Court will be arrested immediately and has the worst to fear as soon as the Bolsheviks take Vienna into their possession ... I myself fall asleep without remorse and have had all the beautiful things life has to offer".

11 With regard to the villa in Breitenstein Alma Mahler-Werfel's ownership was again registered in the cadastral register as a result of a legally binding decision of the Regional State Court for Civil Matters [Landesgericht für Zivilrechtssachen] Vienna from 17 January 1947; File number 25 Cg 39/47.

"German property."[12]/[13] The RC thus followed the argument of the *Finanzprokuratur*, which claimed that the Republic of Austria was not the right defendant since the paintings held by the Austrian Gallery were not considered Austrian but German property. Quite astonishingly the two lay judges overruled the professional judge on this point in the Court of First Instance. The Chairman, Dr Ehrenzweig, who certainly regarded the paintings as Austrian property since they had been acquired in the context of the Gallery's museum administration and had thus become part of an entirety of objects (namely the Austrian Gallery) that was to be considered Austrian property, had not been able to convince the two lay judges of his legal view. Nevertheless, he immediately expressed his contrary opinion in a legal essay, from which Mahler-Werfel's lawyer could – successfully, as we will see – cite the corresponding passages in his appeal.[14]

The reasoning of the ruling also contains an extensive analysis indicating that, in the opinion of the RC Vienna, the restitution claim would have been admitted on its merits and was merely unenforceable because of lacking a tangible defendant. In other words, the political persecution of Mahler-Werfel was accepted, as was the existence of an invalid withdrawal of property, while the independence of the purchase from the National Socialists' takeover of power was expressly negated. The free evaluation of evidence largely followed the statements given by Mahler-Werfel and her witnesses Wilhelm Legler[15] and Ida Wagner-Gebauer.[16]

2. The First Ruling of the Upper Restitution Commission (URC) in 1948

As a result of Mahler-Werfel's administrative appeal of 28 October 1948, a ruling of the URC Vienna (Rkb 1116/48) was issued on 23 Novem-

---

12 As a result of Austria's status as an occupied state the RC was prevented from ruling on "German property" (which the Soviet Union wanted to confiscate as war reparation payments).
13 63 Rk 364/47 = order number 19, file p. 73 - 77; chaired by Dr Adolf Ehrenzweig.
14 Adolf Ehrenzweig, 'Das Deutsche Eigentum', *Juristische Blätter* (1948), p. 472 ff. There it states (p. 473): "One could assume more generally that the Republic of Austria has the position as a party to the dispute in all legal disputes concerning parts of an Austrian entirety of objects. If, for example, an Authority Court in the *Ostmark* has bought a chair and somebody assumes to have a claim to it, he or she should not have to wait for the State Treaty, but should be able to sue the Republic of Austria for its return now."
15 The architect Wilhelm Legler was Alma Mahler-Werfel's nephew and Carl Moll's step-grandson. During the trial he was subsequently nominated as a witness by Alma Mahler-Werfel, quite often in order to testify on internal family matters. The opposing party tried to undermine Legler's credibility by insinuating that he was disappointed not to have received anything from Moll's estate.
16 Ida Wagner-Gebauer had worked as a nanny in the Mahler-Werfel household for many years.

ber 1948, by which the RC's decision was remanded and the matter was referred back to the Court of First Instance.

The URC agreed with the claimant's view regarding the capacity of the Republic of Austria to be a defendant and qualified the adverse argument put by the *Finanzprokuratur* and the RC as "surprising" and "unfounded". The URC emphasized that the Federal Law regarding the "Reunification of Austria with the German Reich" [*Bundesgesetz über die Wiedervereinigung Österreichs mit dem Deutschen Reich*], (BGBl [*Federal Law Gazette*] No. 75/1939) resulted in the former property of the Republic of Austria becoming property of the German Reich but that, on the other hand, the proclamation of independence on 27 April 1945 (StGBl [*State Law Gazette*] No. 1/1945) meant that "the German Reich's property on the national territory of the Republic of Austria became property of the Republic of Austria." On the subject of the Austrian Gallery, it is stated that "none of the occupying powers had stretched out their hands at these treasures, however disputed the concept of the so-called German property might otherwise be."

Less favourable for Alma Mahler-Werfel was the subsequent analysis put forward by the URC Vienna. The obiter admittance of the claim on its merits by the RC Vienna was put into doubt by the URC. In its remission the appellate body gave various instructions for the further proceedings, boiling down to an anticipated evaluation of evidence with a strong bias against Alma Mahler-Werfel's claim.

Regarding *Rocky coast near Ragusa*, the URC stated that this painting had been acquired by the Austrian Gallery as a result of a last will, made on 13 April 1945.[17] "The acquisition therefore in any case takes place at a time when the Republic of Austria was already re-established and is in connection with the destruction, but not the takeover of power by National Socialism, nor the fact, that the applicant was married to a Jew." The URC then reminded the RC that in restitution proceedings "the facts of the case essential for the decision shall be established ex officio" and urged the RC to

---

17 The URC thereby followed the Austrian Gallery's argumentation (contested by Mahler-Werfel), which was based on an acquisition from a legacy of Carl Moll or his son-in-law, Dr Eberstaller.
Dr Eberstaller's last will from 11 April 1945, also signed by his wife, was the matter of a lawsuit between Alma Mahler-Werfel and Anton Klement, Rosa Tamassy, Josef Reiner and Karl Sieber, the persons considered in the last will, in which Mahler-Werfel claimed the nullity of the will (21 Cg 294/47). This dispute supposedly ended on 16 October 1951 (after the Upper Regional State Court Vienna had decided in favour of Alma Mahler-Werfel) with a settlement, according to which the four defendants were to be considered only as legatees. Finally the property was transferred to Alma Mahler-Werfel and Wilhelm Legler as the heirs of Carl Moll (document confirming the transfer [*Einantwortungsurkunde*] dating 24 April 1954) and Marie Eberstaller's (document confirming the transfer dating 23 June 1954). Dr Theodor Eberstaller was the heir of his brother, Dr Richard Eberstaller (document confirming the transfer dating 23 June 1954).

consult the applicant's mother's estate files, "which may show that the painting, irrespective of the dedication as a loan by the applicant [Mahler-Werfel], was actually in the ownership of Jakob Emil Schindler's widow [Anna Moll]."[18]

With respect to the Munch painting, the URC did not regard the matter as ready for decision either:

> "In the ruling [of the RC] it is not regarded as evident that the sale of this painting would have taken place irrespective of the National Socialist takeover of power. The Restitution Commission, however, owes a justification for this assumption.... It has not come to the fore that the claimant being of Jewish kin [sic] at the time of the painting's sale had been exposed to persecution of any kind, particularly concerning her property."

In the following the RC's appraisal of evidence is harshly criticized, revealing the personal views of the judges at the URC. "It is improper – merely based on the testimony of the witness Legler – to accuse of plundering the claimant highly respected personalities such as the painter and outstanding art expert Professor Carl Moll, a man generally held in high esteem and respectable into old age, or the Vice President of the Regional State Court for Criminal Matters, Dr Eberstaller, and his wife, who have departed life voluntarily merely because of the collapse of their political ideals."

The procurement of the estate files of Dr. Eberstaller and his wife was encouraged, and the presumption was that these would show that the villa in Breitenstein, the repair of which was funded by the sales proceeds of the Munch painting, was merely given in trust. On this point the URC added a further speculation: "If the house was transferred to the Eberstaller couple as trustees, the allegation that the claimant had equally entrusted them with custody of her remaining property becomes highly probable." Conclusion by the URC Vienna: "The facts on the request of restitution should undergo legal evaluation according to section 4 *para* 1 of the Third Restitution Act and section 367 Austrian General Civil Code [*Allgemeines Bürgerliches Gesetzbuch, ABGB*]."

In retrospect, this already definitively decided the matter regarding the Munch painting. The case continued for years, but with respect to the Munch painting it eventually ended in 1953 in exactly the same way as the URC had indicated in its 1948 ruling. The URC again conducted an evaluation of the evidence in a very favourable manner for the Republic and

---

18 Anna Moll, *née* Bergen, widow of Schindler, died in 1938; as later became clear, the estate proceedings were discontinued due to a lack of funds, although, according to Alma Mahler-Werfel, there existed "valuable jewellery and securities worth RM 100,000." (63 RK 1372/48 - 86, p. 3 = Rk 216/61, AS 323).

affirmed the acquisition of the Munch painting in good faith "in terms of section 4" of the Third Restitution Act.

3. First Ruling of the Supreme Restitution Commission in 1949 (dismissed)

The revision appeal by the *Finanzprokuratur* (which had not succeeded in its argumentation regarding German property) was rejected by the *Oberste Rückstellungskommission* (Supreme Restitution Commission) on 8 January 1949 because the amount in dispute did not exceed ATS 15,000.[19]

4. Second Ruling of the RC in 1953

With a written submission on 7 April 1950, the continued proceedings at the RC Vienna were extended to the request for restitution of five further paintings by Schindler, namely *Forest Road in the Salzkammergut, Moonrise in the Prater, Hacking Meadow, Cottonwood Alley* and *From Corfu*.[20]

The trial before the RC Vienna – after extensive preliminary proceedings, including the questioning of numerous witnesses – finally ended on 9 April 1953 with a ruling fully recognizing Mahler-Werfel's claim.[21] The Federal Republic of Austria was ordered to restitute to Alma Mahler-Werfel the paintings *Summer Night on the Beach* by Edvard Munch as well as *Rocky Coast near Ragusa, Moonrise in the Prater, Hacking Meadow, Cottonwood Alley* and *From Corfu* by Jakob Emil Schindler.

In the description of the facts of the case it is assumed that all the paintings were owned by the claimant. Professor Grimschitz' statement, according to which *Moonrise in the Prater* and *Hacking Meadow* were Moll's property, was not followed, "since this witness was no closer to the family background than the witness Legler," whose claim that these paintings all belonged to the claimant was thus preferred.[22]

---

19 Decision Rkv 219/48. According to section 21 *para* 2 Third Restitution Act a (revision) appeal to the SRC against a URC ruling because of incorrect legal assessment is only admissible if the amount in dispute exceeds ATS 15,000. An appeal against an affirming ruling of the URC is furthermore only admissible if the URC regards the appeal to the SRC as admissible.
20 Motion to take evidence, order number 31 AS 116.
21 63 RK 1372/48, order number 91.
22 The art historian Bruno Grimschitz was a multi-functionary in the art and museums field during National Socialism: he was not only the director of the Modern Gallery and the Gallery of the 19th Century (today Austrian Gallery in the Belvedere), but also head of the painting gallery of the Art Historical Museum and the Prince-Eugene-Museum, professor of art history and museums as well as head of the Gaumuseum in Salzburg (towards the end of the war). In this latter capacity he was also involved in opaque dealings with the art dealer Friedrich Welz in Salzburg; cf Gert Kerschbaumer, *Meister des Verwirrens. Die Geschäfte des Kunsthändlers Friedrich Welz* (Wien 2000) p. 43 ff, as well as Monika Mayer, 'Bruno Grimschitz und die Österreichische Galerie

The legal assessment described the fact that the claimant, as the wife of Franz Werfel, who was a Jew according to the National Socialist Nuremberg Laws, was subject to political persecution as "self-evident". Express or tacit authorization of Eberstaller or another person to sell the paintings was not taken as proved, neither was an entrusting of the objects.

The sale of the paintings through the claimant was deemed a withdrawal in terms of the Third Restitution Act. It was added that, "The use of the sales revenue for the repair of the house is irrelevant for this question. It might only serve as the basis for claims of an agent of necessity (*negotiorum gestor*), but the fact that Eberstaller used the house together with his family, that he received the rent payments for the house and that the costs of the repair were comparatively insignificant are arguments against this possibility."[23] Apart from that, a testament (of Eberstaller or the Molls) would, as a transaction concerning somebody else's assets, be irrelevant.

The ruling, which in the light of the extensive preliminary proceedings is rather short in its evaluation of evidence, would have meant a total victory for Alma Mahler-Werfel. Sure enough, however, it did not become legally binding since the *Finanzprokuratur* appealed and won in the next instance, at least regarding the Munch painting.

5. Second Ruling of the URC in 1953

In its ruling of 16 June 1953 (Rkb 186/53), the URC at the Upper Regional State Court in Vienna rejected the restitution claim for the Munch painting following the Republic of Austria's appeal, but did not deem the matter ready for a decision with respect to the Schindler paintings, thus referring the case back to the Court of First Instance for further proceedings.

First of all the ruling dealt with the evaluation of evidence in great detail, highlighting those aspects of the witnesses' testimonies that were favourable to Moll and the Eberstallers. Emphasis was placed on the statements by painting colleagues and friends of Moll and his business partners in the Gallery of the 19th Century; of the claimant's witnesses only those passages in their statements speaking against the possibility of fraudulent behaviour by Moll and the Eberstallers were cited. All in all, the alleged harmony between Alma Mahler-Werfel and the three people who committed suicide was emphasized.[24]

1938 – 1945', in: G. Anderl & A. Caruso (eds.), *NS-Kunstraub in Österreich und die Folgen* (Innsbruck 2005), p. 59 ff.
23 63 Rk 1372/48 - 91, p. 5.
24 In her statement before the RC Vienna as well as in her autobiography (*Mein Leben*, p. 275) Mahler-Werfel says about Moll: "He had always been my archenemy."

The fact that the URC would pay particular attention to the reputation of Moll and the Eberstallers had already become clear in its first ruling[25] and was now reconfirmed. Furthermore the legal view already outlined in the first URC ruling regarding the Gallery of the 19th Century's acquisition of the Munch painting in good faith was readopted.

As the result of its own evaluation, the URC assumed that "Professor Moll or Mrs Eberstaller or the two of them together [sic] were authorized to dispose of the painting in question since it had been entrusted to them."[26] The URC considered it to be in accordance with "logical thinking" that Alma Mahler-Werfel not only entrusted the house in Breitenstein [note: including the fixtures] to her half-sister, but also the "disposal over the [note: what was obviously meant was 'other'] moveable assets".

However, the idea that "Moll or Mrs Eberstaller or the two of them together" actually had authorization (a fact that had been contested by the claimant throughout the trial) did not seem to be assumed by the URC Vienna since it subsumed the acquisition of the Munch painting under section 4 of the Third Restitution Act, which, in comparison to section 367 of the Austrian General Civil Code, was a slightly modified provision regarding the acquisition of moveable assets in good faith. It thus took the Munch painting to be a withdrawn object in terms of the Third Restitution Act, which did not, however, have to be restituted since the Gallery had acquired the painting in good faith (i.e. was unaware that it had been withdrawn).

As far as the good faith of the Gallery is concerned, the following remarks by the URC can be found: "As the Austrian Gallery then [i.e. 18 March 1938 – date of the handing over of the painting to Moll] trusted him [i.e. Moll] without any proof of authorization to receive five paintings from the claimant [i.e. the loan by Mahler-Werfel], they could arguably equally trust him when he subsequently sold one of these paintings in order to repair the roof of the house, which, despite the donation in the form of a trust, still belonged to the claimant."[27] In other words, since the Gallery gave the entrusted paintings to a member of the family of the owner, who had fled abroad, without authorization by the owner, the good faith of the Gallery is accepted when the daughter of this family member later sold one of these paintings – again without any proof of authorization.

The URC concluded that, with regard to the Munch paintings, there was no obligation of restitution in accordance with section 4 Third Restitution Act: "The representatives of the Austrian Gallery were well aware that they were dealing with assets of a victim of political persecution, but they could not detect an act of withdrawal, but a transaction to which this person – the

---

25 As to Moll's general esteem, it should be noted that he had been an honorary citizen of the City of Vienna since 1931.
26 Rkb 186/53 = Rk 216/61, file p. 380.
27 Rkb 186/53 = Rk 216/61, file p. 380.

seller – was entitled. Therefore, the restitution claim with regard to the painting by Edvard Munch is rejected."[28] Nevertheless, the URC Vienna added that "due to the above mentioned correspondence between Professor Moll and Dr Schwarz[29] (an employee of the Gallery of the 19th century) … it [can] quite safely be assumed to be evident that the sale of the painting would also have taken place irrespective of the takeover of power."[30]

6. Second Ruling of the SRC in 1953 (dismissed)

Alma Mahler-Werfel's appeal for revision was again rejected by the SRC on formal grounds since the amount in dispute did not exceed ATS 15,000. Thus the ruling of the URC became legally binding in respect of the Munch painting.

7. Further Proceedings

In the course of the further proceedings, oral hearings before the RC took place only sporadically. Alma Mahler-Werfel and her representatives remained, however, in contact with the Austrian authorities in order to try to achieve the restitution of the Munch painting by extrajudicial means.[31] Through such out-of-court negotiations Mahler-Werfel achieved the restitution of *Rocky Coast near Ragusa* and *Cottonwood Alley*.[32]

On the occasion of an enquiry by the RC Vienna on 31 March 1961, Alma Mahler-Werfel declared to "maintain the asserted claims since a settlement had not been reached despite certain approximations."[33] A request for judicial assistance was made to the Austrian Consulate General on 18 September 1964 for a hearing of Alma Mahler-Werfel in New York (her

---

28 Rkb 186/53 = Rk 216/61, file p. 381.
29 The URC hereby refers to letters from 1 March and 4 March 1938 (annexes H and G), in which Moll negotiated the sale of the Munch paintings in Alma Mahler-Werfel's name. The authorization claimed by Moll in the letter dating 4 March 1938 was denied by Alma Mahler-Werfel in the restitution proceedings.
30 Rkb 186/53 = Rk 216/61, file p. 381. Regarding the Schindler paintings the matter was remanded to the RC for a new trial by the URC.
31 Oral proceedings were held on 20 January 1954, 21 September 1961 and 6 March 1964.
32 The restitution of the paintings *Rocky Coast near Ragusa* and *Cottonwood Alley* was effected as a result of a regulation of the Federal Ministry of Education Zl.28.989.II/6/54 on 19 February 1954.
    Regarding the *Forest Road in Scharfling*, restitution had already taken place on 4 August 1948 (according to order number 96 file p. 384 in the context of the proceedings 63 Rk 30/50), and so the claim in this regard was withdrawn.
33 Statement from 2.5.1961, Rk 216/61 order number 126 volume II file number 5.

last visit to Austria was in 1947). Alma Mahler-Werfel died on 11 December 1964 before being interrogated.[34]

D. Restitution Request by Marina Mahler in 1999

The Commission of Provenance Research in Austrian Federal Museums [*Kommission zur Erforschung der Provenienzen in den Österreichischen Bundesmuseen*] was established by the Federal Ministry of Education and Culture in early 1998 with the assignment "to systematically file the art objects acquired in the period in question to resolve all questions regarding the ownership during the National Socialist period and the immediate post-war era."

In March 1999 Marina Mahler received a dossier from this commission on the acquisition of Munch's *Summer Night on the Beach* prepared by the art historian Monika Mayer. Marina Mahler consequently requested restitution of the Munch painting, but abstained from claiming restitution of the Schindler paintings as ownership by Alma Mahler-Werfel could not be proved.

In April 1999 the final 37-page report of the Commission of Provenance Research was presented to the Art Restitution Advisory Board. The report chronologically listed the events, starting with Alma Mahler-Werfel's lending of the painting to the Austrian Gallery on 2 August 1937 up to Alma's death in New York on 11 December 1964. In her résumé[35] Monika Mayer pointed out that the allegedly 'bona fide' purchase of the painting from Marie Eberstaller (Alma's half-sister) in 1940 should be viewed in the context that "the ownership right of Alma Mahler-Werfel was known to the Austrian Gallery," and referred to the witness statement of former director Bruno Grimschitz[36] in the restitution proceedings. Furthermore, as to any possible intentions to sell before 1938, she records the fact that there was no proof of authorization or written authorization by Mahler-Werfel to sell the Munch painting; not even an agreement to interrupt the loan had been received – the painting, after all, had been taken back in 1938 by Carl Moll, Marie Eberstaller's father and Alma's stepfather.

However in its session on 27 October 1999 the Advisory Board "owing to a clear and unambiguous legal situation" saw itself unable to recommend a transfer of ownership of the Munch painting to Alma Mahler-Werfel's legal successor.

The basis for the Advisory Board's legal assessment was first and foremost the file of the *Finanzprokuratur* regarding the proceedings under the

---

34 The last document in the proceedings is a decision by the judge to wait for the result of the testamentary proceedings.
35 Dossier of the Commission of Provenance Research in the Austrian Federal Museums by Monika Mayer (1999) pp. 35 - 36.
36 For Grimschitz see footnote 22 above.

Third Restitution Act in the post-war period that Alma Mahler-Werfel, who had suffered losses as the owner, had instigated.[37]

The decisions made by the authorities during the post-war era were subject to evaluation by the Advisory Board: The ruling of the Restitution Commission at the Regional Court for Civil Matters Vienna of 9 April 1953,[38] which obliged the Republic of Austria to restitute the painting, was only briefly mentioned and the "extremely cursory evaluation of evidence by the first instance" criticized. According to the Advisory Board's opinion the decision in first instance "almost completely" lacked "a legal assessment of the stated facts of the case."

The Upper Restitution Commission at the Upper Regional Court Vienna, in its ruling of 16 June 1953,[39] as the second instance, had by contrast complied with the complaint of the *Finanzprokuratur* and dismissed Alma Mahler-Werfel's request for restitution "because of a detailed evaluation of evidence" – this being the Advisory Board's evaluation. The Advisory Board cites from the decision:

> "After all the house in Breitenstein had equally been given to Maria Eberstaller as a gift only in the form of a trust – it has now already been restituted – and the consequence, that the applicant [Alma] had not only entrusted her [Marie Eberstaller] with the real estate, but also with the disposal over the moveable assets, corresponds to logical thinking … Therefore the Restitution Commission, despite the contrary statement of witness Arch. Legler, takes as granted that the paintings can be considered entrusted to Prof. Moll or Maria Eberstaller. In the sense of the provision section 4 of the Third Restitution Act there is no obligation to restitution in this case …The representatives of the Austrian Gallery were well aware that they were dealing with the property of a political refugee, however they could not view this as an act of expropriation, but as the legitimate disposal by the seller … As a result of the above mentioned correspondence between Prof. Moll and Dr. Schwarz it can unobjectionably be taken for granted that it would have come to the selling of the painting irrespective of the takeover of power".

As a result of these elaborations of the Upper Restitution Commission Vienna, the Art Restitution Advisory Board came to the conclusions formulated in point 3: In other words, the dismissal of the request for restitu-

---

37 For the decision on the restitution claims according to the Third, Fifth and Sixth Restitution Act, restitution commissions set up at each regional court [*Landesgericht*] were assigned with carrying out jurisdiction in civil law matters. Altogether three stages of appeal were envisaged. In the second instance, upper restitution commissions decided. The third and last instance was the Supreme Restitution Commission set up at the Supreme Court [*OGH*]. For details of the practice of these commissions see Franz-Stefan Meissel, Thomas Olechowski & Christoph Gnant, *Untersuchungen zur Praxis der Verfahren vor den Rückstellungskommissionen* (Wien-München 2004).
38 File number 63 RK 1373/48-91.
39 File number Rkb 186/53-95.

tion by Alma Mahler-Werfel was legally binding (*res iudicata*) and every court was consequently bound by the ruling of the Upper Restitution Commission, which had stated "the legally effective non-appealability of the acquisition of property by the Federation." An elimination of the formal and material legal effects of the ruling could only be considered if there were causes for a retrial in the sense of section 530 ff ZPO [*Code of Civil Procedure*]. It could not be the Advisory Board's task to give a recommendation contradicting a legally binding ruling. The requirements of section 1 clause 2 Art Restitution Act, which would allow for a restitution recommendation, were not fulfilled since, regarding the Munch painting, it had been "stated with legal effect that the requirements for the restitution provision were not met and that therefore there was no incriminated legal act according to the Annulment Act."

Second Section: Legal Analysis

The following section is an analysis of the Art Restitution Act 1998 (A.) and the proceedings regarding the Munch painting submitted to the Art Restitution Advisory Board on the basis of this Act (B.). The reasons behind the Advisory Board's decision will be subjected to a legal evaluation, with particular attention being paid to the interpretation of section 1 clause 2 Art Restitution Act 1998.[40] An assessment of the case, however, also requires a critical analysis of the 1953 decision of the URC Vienna (C.) and consideration of the legal evaluations regarding the nullity of extremely unjust decisions. These considerations have since become part of the General Settlement Fund Law [*EntschädigungsfondsG*] 2001 (D.), in the light of which a re-evaluation of the case is advisable.

A) Art Restitution Act 1998

Based on the Commission for Provenance Research's results the Art Restitution Act 1998 provides for three categories of restitution authorizations for art objects that passed into the ownership of Federal museums and collections during the Nazi regime or the post-war era.[41]

a. Section 1 clause 1 Art Restitution Act 1998 covers art objects that were withheld in the course of proceedings under the Export Ban Act [*AusfuhrverbotsG*] (StGBl No. 18/1918) and passed into the possession of Austrian museums and collections as 'gifts' or 'dedications'. This provision refers to art objects that were gratuitously transferred to an Austrian museum as a countermove to export approval after 8 May 1945. From

---

40 The following parts are largely based on the legal opinion that I gave in December 2005 at the request of Marina Mahler, granddaughter and legal successor of Alma Mahler-Werfel.
41 Parliamentary Materials (1464 Blg NR XX.GP 1).

today's point of view – in the opinion of the legislative body – "the then chosen procedure is unjustifiable",[42] and the competent Federal Minister is appropriately authorized to transfer property to the original owner.

b. Section 1 clause 2 Art Restitution Act 1998 concerns art objects that "rightfully passed into the ownership of the Federation" but were the object of a legal transaction that is void according to the Annulment Act [*Nichtigkeits G*] 1946. Acquisitions of art works that had been the object of a void withdrawal of property during the Nazi regime, i.e. specifically all cases of 'aryanization', are subject to this regulation.

c. Section 1 clause 3 Art Restitution Act 1998 in contrast covers art objects that, despite a restitution procedure, could not be returned to the original owners or their heirs and have passed into the ownership of the Federation as ownerless objects.[43]

According to section 2 *para* 2 Art Restitution Act the Federal Ministers in the cases covered by section 1 Art Restitution Act are authorized to make a transfer to the original owner or their legal successor after hearing the advice of the Art Restitution Advisory Board set up by the Federal Ministry of Education and Culture (now: Federal Ministry of Education, Science and Culture).

No request is needed for an art work to be examined by the Advisory Board; the procedure is governed by the official 'inquisitorial' system. The General Administrative Procedure Act [*Allgemeines Verwaltungsverfahrens G (AVG)*] is not applicable as its applicability was not provided for in the Art Restitution Act.[44] As a consequence there is no provision for the procedural rights of the parties.[45] Moreover section 2 *para* 2 Art Restitution Act expressly excludes any entitlement to claim transfer of property, although there is no doubt that the authorities are bound to the principle of objectivity under constitutional law and that, in the case of unequal treatment, a claim can be filed with the competent court.[46]

---

42 Parliamentary Materials (1464 Blg NR XX.GP 1).
43 According to section 2 *para* 1 clause 2 Art Restitution Act 1998 art objects of this kind may be transferred to the National Fund of the Republic of Austria for Victims of National Socialism [*Nationalfonds der Republik Österreich für Opfer des Nationalsozialismus*] for use by the Fund. As the restitution reports published by the Federal Ministry of Education and Culture show, this authorization has never been used.
44 The catalogue of Art II *para* 2 EGVG does not mention the Art Restitution Act. See also Noll, *Juridikum* 1 (2003), p. 33. The Green Party [*Grüne*] had demanded a corresponding amendment during their coalition talks with the Austrian People's Party [*ÖVP*], which – like the coalition talks as a whole – failed.
45 The Supreme Administrative Court [*VwGH*] accordingly decided (rejection decision B 422/00-4 of 30 June 2000) that the letter by Federal Minister Elisabeth Gehrer, in which Marina Mahler was denied restitution, constituted official notification.
46 In this connection the Supreme Court's *Bundesbetreuungserkenntnisse* (1 Ob 272/02 k and 9 Ob 71/03 m) should be remembered, in which the existence of actionable civil claims is derived from the principle of objectivity even in cases of voluntary benefits

B) The Munch Painting in the light of section 1 clause 2 Art Restitution Act

1. The elements of section 1 clause 2 Art Restitution Act 1998

In the question of the restitution of *Summer Night on the Beach* the Advisory Board mainly focused on clause 2 of section 1 Art Restitution Act, which is examined in detail below. According to the Board, a gratuitous retransfer of property is possible for those art objects in Austrian Federal museums and collections "that have rightly passed into the ownership of the Federation, but were beforehand the object of a legal transaction according to section 1 of the Federal Law of 15 May 1946 on the nullity of legal transactions and other legal acts that happened during the German occupation of Austria, *passed into the ownership of the Republic of Austria* (note: not in italics in the original) BGBl No. 106/1946 and are still in the ownership of the Federation."

The wording of section 1 clause 2 Art Restitution Act 1998 is undoubtedly misconceived. The additional subordinate clause "passed into the ownership of the Republic of Austria" (in italics above), for instance, is nonsensical and should be ignored as an editing mistake.[47] Beyond that the provision is generally too comprehensive as, according to the text, it must be applied to all art objects that were subject to expropriation during National Socialism and then became Federal property. This would also cover all cases specifically governed by section 1 clause 1 Art Restitution Act (i.e. acquisitions of restituted art objects from their owners in the context of export authorizations). In order not to make section 1 clause 1 Art Restitution Act redundant, a systematic interpretation requires the provisions of clause 2 of section 1 Art Restitution Act to be applied to withdrawn art objects acquired from third persons (and not from the *in rem* authorized person as in clause 1).[48]

Nevertheless it must be stated that section 1 clause 2 Art Restitution Act is to be understood as a general clause allowing for the restitution of art works owned by the Federation and that had been the object of a void legal

---

granted by the Federation within the framework of the Commitment Act [*SelbstbindungsG*].
47 R. Welser & Chr. Rabl, *Der Fall Klimt* (Wien 2005), p. 98 footnote 105; cf. on the internet under www.adele.at; see also the legal opinion of the *Finanzprokuratur* (Vice president Manfred Kremser) on the restitution matter of Adele Bloch-Bauer, which can also be downloaded from www.adele.at.
48 Welser & Rabl, *Der Fall Klimt*, p. 103.

transaction in the sense of the Annulment Act 1946 and were not restituted.[49]

It follows from the preparatory legislative documents [*Gesetzesmaterialien*] of the Art Restitution Act 1998 that clause 2 is aimed at cases in which the Federation has in good faith acquired art objects that had been withdrawn from victims of National Socialism. This includes cases in which the Federation had acquired aryanized art objects at auctions or bought them in the market and only later learned that they were loot. In such situations, Austrian civil law allows the acquisition of property in good faith according to section 367 Austrian General Civil Code or section 4 of the Third Restitution Act 1947, so that an acquisition of rights to the disadvantage of victims of National Socialism was possible.

The illustrating documents [*Erläuterungen*] comment on this matter as follows:

> "Some museum directors had acquired art objects in good faith from authorized dealers in the art market (in the post-war era) and doubts regarding their provenance had only arisen at a later date."[50]

Such acquisitions, which are incontestable under current law, but are nevertheless tainted with the odour of profiting from the expropriation of victims of National Socialism, were intended to be cancelled by section 1 clause 2 Art Restitution Act 1998.

The text of Section 1 clause 2 Art Restitution Act 1998 takes up the elements of section 1 Annulment Act 1946. As a consequence the art object must have been "the object of a legal transaction during the German occupation of Austria, effected in connection with the economic or political penetration, designed to withdraw property or property rights from natural or legal persons who were entitled to these rights on 13 March 1938."[51]

The fact that the Annulment Act 1946 itself did not lead to any legal consequences at the time, since its section 2 expressly stated that the form, assertion and extent of claims arising from section 1 would be governed by another Federal law, is in this context irrelevant. Section 1 clause 2 Art Restitution Act 1998 takes up the elements of the general provision of section 1 Annulment Act 1946 and cannot be viewed as a reference to legal

---

49 Georg Graf, 'Überlegungen zum Anwendungsbereich des § 1 Z 2 KunstrückgabeG', *Notariatszeitung* (2005), p. 323, who rightly draws attention to the fact that section 1 clause 2 must be seen as a general clause with a conceivably wide scope of application.
50 Parliamentary Materials (1390 Blg NR XX.GP 4).
51 Federal Law from 15 May 1946, BGBl No. 106, on the declaration of nullity of legal transactions and other legal actions effected during the German occupation of Austria (Annulment Act); printed and commented in: Ludwig Viktor Heller, Wilhelm Rauscher & Rudolf St. Baumann, *Gesetz über die Erfassung arisierter und anderer entzogener Vermögenschaften, Vermögensentziehungsanmeldeverordnung, Nichtigkeitsgesetz, Erstes Rückstellungsgesetz*, 2nd edition (Wien 1947), p. 40 ff.

consequences. The fact that the legal consequences of nullity were postponed through the reservation of particular provisions, and the fact that the nullity of the legal transaction in the sense of the Annulment Act was merely relative[52] and had to be asserted by the damaged owner, must not be considered in the legal evaluation of whether a matter was the object of a legal transaction in the sense of section 1 Annulment Act 1946.[53]

In the post-war era, the respective provisions of the Restitution Acts, substantiated by the Annulment Act, obviously had to be consulted to decide on the question of a particular restitution obligation. The term of a void legal transaction (section 1 Annulment Act 1946) was defined more clearly for the purposes of restituting withdrawn property under the Third Restitution Act 1947. According to section 1 *para* 1 of the Third Restitution Act, the property had to be withdrawn from the owner (authorized person) during the German occupation of Austria, either by an unauthorized action or based on laws or other orders, in particular also by legal transactions or other legal acts connected to the National Socialists' takeover of power. A withdrawal of property had to be assumed if the owner was subject to political persecution by the National Socialists and the purchaser of the property was unable to convince a court that the transfer of property would equally have taken place irrespective of the takeover by National Socialists.

In the case of such a withdrawal of property in the sense of the Third Restitution Act the damaged person could request the Restitution Commission to order restitution of the withdrawn property, unless the other party could prove that the object had been acquired in good faith according to section 4 *para* 1 of the Third Restitution Act. In this way the legislative body of the post-war era sought to protect the interests of transaction security and the acquisition in good faith in specific cases.

2. Munch's *Summer Night on the Beach* and section 1 clause 2 Art Restitution Act 1998

Regarding *Summer Night on the Beach* the question arises as to whether the negative decision on a restitution claim under the Third Restitution Act, resulting from the assumption of an acquisition in good faith under section 4 *para* 1 Third Restitution Act, means that the act of acquisition could not be regarded as an action of withdrawal. The Advisory Board and, following its opinion, the Federal Ministry of Education and Culture started from this assumption, given that the restitution report 2000/2001 refers to the state-

---

52 Compare in detail G. Graf, *Die österreichische Rückstellungsgesetzgebung* (Wien-München 2003), p. 41.
53 According to the opinion of Welser & Rabl, *Der Fall Klimt*, p. 101, section 1 Annulment Act 1946 represents "an independent condition for the applicability of section 1 clause 2 Restitution Act 1998, so that the applicability of one of the former Restitution Acts is not necessary."

ment by the Restitution Commission in the restitution procedure at that time "that the acquisition of property by the Austrian Gallery had not been the result of an act of withdrawal." This means that it was stated, with legal effect, that the elements of an act of withdrawal, and thus of an incriminated legal action according to the Annulment Act, were not fulfilled.

a. In this context some general remarks concerning the nature and effects of being legally binding ('*Bindungswirkung*') are necessary. It is undisputed that the 1953 decision in which the URC Vienna dismissed the claim was legally binding. Consequently a claim for restitution of the painting based on the Third Restitution Act – not taking into account the theoretical[54] possibility of a retrial under section 530 Code of Civil Procedure – was no longer possible. In no way, however, do the legal effects with regard to this basis for a claim pursuant to the Third Restitution Act exclude a possible obligation to restitute the Munch painting *as a result of another basis for a claim*, particularly the Art Restitution Act 1998, which was enacted several decades later. The fact that a legally binding decision ascertaining the acquisition of property never excludes voluntary restitution is equally clear.[55]

In other words: a legally binding decision based on pre-war law cannot be used as a basis for excluding restitution under the law in force today if a new base for claims by victims of National Socialism has been created – specifically the Art Restitution Act 1998. It is therefore inexplicable that the Advisory Board, which expressed full moral understanding for Marina Mahler's restitution request, regarded the same request as impossible with respect to a decision based on the legal situation in 1953. Since today's

---

54 Under jurisdiction in the post-war era, the applicability of section 530 Code of Civil Procedure to proceedings under the Third Restitution Act had of course been denied since these were non-dispute proceedings [*Außerstreitverfahren*]. Although a retrial would certainly be accepted by jurisdiction (JBl 1998, p. 731 *Klicka* = ecolex 1998, p. 833 *Oberhammer*), the absolute time limits set in section 530 Code of Civil Procedure have usually already expired for proceedings under the Third Restitution Act.

55 Cf. Graf, 'Überlegungen zum Anwendungsbereich des § 1 Z 2 KunstrückgabeG', NZ (2005), p. 330 sq Fn 38 [*translation*]: "If in a proceeding the plaintiff is granted property in an object with legally binding effects, these material legal effects of the judgement do not bar him or her from nevertheless leaving the object with the defendant or giving it to him or her after a certain period of time. The material legal effects do not hinder the person benefiting from the decision in question to show behaviour corresponding to the legal point of view of the opposite side. If, therefore, new facts have come to the fore since the taking of the decision by the Restitution Commission, nothing – and particularly not the material legal effects – would bar the Republic from behaving according to the new standard of knowledge and giving back the painting. Neither does the Art Restitution Act prohibit such a restitution."

It should be noted that not only new facts, but also a *new legal position* has to be taken into account and that if the prerequisites of the Art Restitution Act are fulfilled, restitution is not only possible but actually *compulsory*. If this obligation is not fulfilled, even civil *damage claims* are possible!

standards, where the Republic is considered to have joint responsibility for the injustices created by National Socialism, are to a large extent manifested in the Art Restitution Act 1998, today's legal situation is also considerably different from that prevailing in 1953.

b. It would obviously be possible for the decision taken then to still be binding regarding an element of the provision of the Art Restitution Act. And this was obviously the Art Restitution Advisory Board's opinion since it assumed that the then dismissal of the application for restitution of the Munch painting meant, with legally binding effect, that the painting had not been the object of a legal transaction in the terms of section 1 Annulment Act 1946.

But is this point stated in the 1953 decision of the URC at all? The URC's reason for dismissing the claim was not that there had *not* been a withdrawal of property in the case of the Munch painting. Instead it claimed – irrespective of that! – that the Gallery of the 19th Century has acquired property in good faith according to section 4 *para* 1 of the Third Restitution Act.

In order to answer this question, a more detailed examination of section 4 *para* 1 Third Restitution Act is necessary:

"Were moveable assets acquired at a public auction or in the context of execution or insolvency proceedings or in return for payment from an authorized trader or from persons to whom the owner him or herself had entrusted them for their use, for management or other purposes, then they are only considered withdrawn in the sense of section 1 *para* 1 if the purchaser knew or had to know that the property had been withdrawn."

Already the text of the provision ("if the purchaser knew or had to know that the property had been *withdrawn*") clearly suggests that acquisition in good faith requires a withdrawal.

For the commentators on the Third Restitution Act, Heller/Rauscher/Baumann[56] and – taking up their points – Graf,[57] the scope of applicability of this rule only includes property that has already been withdrawn, and

---

56 Compare Ludwig Viktor Heller, Wilhelm Rauscher & Rudolf Baumann, *Drittes Rückstellungsgesetz*, 2nd edition (Wien 1948), p. 207 [*translation*]: "The privilege pursuant to *para* 1 of section 4 only comes in useful to the purchaser of property that has already been withdrawn (i.e. beforehand). Therefore its version of the text denies the possibility to maintain the validity of the transaction by, for instance, claiming good faith to those who, in the owner's business enterprise, purchased a moveable asset at an unfair price because the owner was forced to sell it at a loss."

57 See Graf, *Rückstellungsgesetzgebung*, p. 215 ff. The Restitution Commission probably interpreted the provision in a different way in certain constellations. However Rkv 91/49 = JBl 1949, p. 360 states that section 4 *para* 1 only privileges the original acquisition from non-owners.

thus not the sale by the damaged owner him or herself. The property must have been the object of a different transaction, which for its part had to qualify as a withdrawal.

The preparatory documents to the Third Restitution Act show that the intention was to introduce a position comparable to the original acquisition of property in section 367 Austrian General Civil Code into the Third Restitution Act for moveable assets.[58] This parallelism[59] gives further insights for the interpretation: The legislative body "like in section 367 Austrian General Civil Code" provided for "a special form of 'original' (i.e. independent of the successor's rights) acquisition of property and therefore, in particular cases of acquisition, a denial of the restitution claim, the vindication."[60] Section 4 *para* 1 Third Restitution Act protects acquisition in good faith or the objectively unsuspicious acquisition of withdrawn property by a non-authorized person analogous to sections 367 ff Austrian General Civil Code.[61] This means that the lack of authorization of the previous holder is 'cured' and that property is acquired in good faith because the legislative body does not permit the effects of the underlying legal defect (in the case of section 367 Austrian General Civil Code: the lack of authorization in *rem*; in the case of section 4 *para* 1 of the Third Restitution Act: the existence of a void withdrawal of property).

It should therefore be noted in respect of section 4 *para* 1 Third Restitution Act that, in all cases, a withdrawal is the prerequisite for the applicability of the provisions on acquisition in good faith. In the case of good faith, an original acquisition of property by the purchaser is possible. In this respect the provision contains an order concerning the *in rem* allocation of property, but does not give any information on the legal quality of the title. This must, however, still be regarded as a withdrawal; it is merely ordered that the legal effects of a withdrawal under the Third Restitution Act – especially the claim to restitution of the originally damaged owner – shall not happen.

There is no doubt, however, that the sale of the Munch painting to the Austrian Gallery (at that time the Gallery of the 19th century) in 1940 constitutes a void legal act in the sense of the Annulment Act. The application of the criteria of the Third Restitution Act leads to the same result. Since Alma Mahler-Werfel was a politically persecuted person, there is only one

---

58 See the explaining remarks to the government proposal in: Heller/Rauscher/Baumann, *Drittes Rückstellungsgesetz*, p. 147, to section 4 [*translation*]: "Here the provisions of section 367 ABGB are extended to other forms of acquisition in the context of execution or insolvency proceedings for practical reasons and reasons of equity."
59 Graf, *Rückstellungsgesetzgebung*, p. 215 ff criticizes the lack of parallelism to the acquisition in good faith according to section 367 ABGB in the starting situations to be regulated and concludes that there was no factual need for a privilege of the acquisition in good faith in the case of restitutions.
60 Heller/Rauscher/Baumann, *Drittes Rückstellungsgesetz*, p. 206.
61 Cf Heller/Rauscher/Baumann: *Drittes Rückstellungsgesetz*, p. 205 ff.

situation in which this would not constitute a withdrawal of property, namely if the specific legal transaction would have taken place in the same manner if the National Socialists had not taken over power. But surely this is not the case.[62]

As an interim résumé it is worth noting that:

a) the legally binding ruling by the Restitution Commission in 1953 merely stated that the painting was the property of the Republic of Austria, but by no means excluded the possibility of a void 'withdrawal of property' in the sense of section 1 Annulment Act to the disadvantage of Alma Mahler-Werfel during the National Socialist period;

b) the contrary view of the Art Restitution Advisory Board inadmissibly mixed the existence of a void legal action in the sense of section 1 Annulment Act with the question of a restitution obligation for objects acquired in good faith under section 4 of the Third Restitution Act; therefore this opinion of the Advisory Board must not be followed;

c) the prerequisites of section 1 clause 2 Art Restitution Act 1998 had certainly been met in the case of the Munch painting *Summer Night on the Beach*.

3. Legally Inadmissible Reasoning of the 1953 Decision of the URC Vienna

The Art Restitution Advisory Board's recommendation not to return the Munch painting to Alma Mahler-Werfel's legal successor was based not only on the argument of the legally binding effects of the 1953 URC decision – above already qualified as unfounded – but also includes an evaluation of the two decisions, which came to different conclusions on this point. The fact that the Advisory Board's recommendation followed the decision in second instance was thus based not only on the legal effectiveness of this decision, but also on the alleged higher *persuasiveness* of the URC's decision in comparison to the 1953 decision in first instance by the RC Vienna, which was in favour of Alma Mahler-Werfel. The Advisory Board uncritically adopted the evaluations, which the appellate body (URC Vienna) in turn used to justify its departure from the decision in first instance. A closer analysis of the decision by the URC Vienna shows, however, that it is by no means better or more convincingly argued than the decision in first instance,

---

62 For the stricter criteria of the *Befreiungsbeweis* ('liberating proof', the proof of the independence of the legal transaction from the National Socialists' takeover of power) see Meissel/Olechowski/Gnant: *Untersuchungen zur Praxis der Verfahren vor den Rückstellungskommissionen*, p. 53 ff, p. 97 ff, p. 144 ff.

which stated that the Munch painting should be restituted to Alma Mahler-Werfel.

The need for an ex-post evaluation of the circumstances regarding the non-restitution arises from the purpose of the Art Restitution Act 1998, which – as the preparatory legislative documents show – specifically also seeks to cover those cases in which the seemingly lawful acquisition of art works by the Republic of Austria is later subject to doubt.[63] The 1953 decision of the URC Vienna will consequently be assessed in terms of its legal 'dubiousness' below.

As elaborated above, the Provenance Research Commission's dossier already expressed doubts about the acquisition in good faith at the time. At least, according to Monika Mayer's résumé, the Austrian Gallery (then the Gallery of the 19th century) had always known that the Munch painting did not belong to Marie Eberstaller or Carl Moll, but to Alma Mahler-Werfel.

Upon closer legal examination, the 1953 decision of the URC Vienna actually turns out to be a downright misjudgement without any conclusive argumentation to support it.

The URC Vienna justifies the non-restitution of the Munch painting by stating that it had been acquired in good faith in accordance with section 4 *para* 1 of the Third Restitution Act, thus meaning there was no obligation of restitution. This central point of the URC's reasoning is subjected to an extensive legal assessment below.

For the prerequisites of section 4 *para* 1 Third Restitution Act[64] to be fulfilled with regard to the case in consideration a) a moveable asset must be acquired, b) in return for remuneration, c) by somebody to whom the owner himself had entrusted it, provided that d) the purchaser did not know (or did not have to know) that the asset had been withdrawn.

Section 4 *para* 1 Third Restitution Act represents a case of denied restitution of a withdrawn object, in which, according to the lawmaker's intention, the provisions of section 367 Austrian General Civil Code, i.e. of original acquisition of property in good faith[65], shall extend[66] to other forms

---

63 The fact that this does not necessarily imply a reproach of wrongdoing on the part of the person acting for the Republic of Austria was convincingly shown by Graf, 'Überlegungen zum Anwendungsbereich des § 1 Z 2 KunstrückgabeG', *NZ* (2005), p. 331 ff.

64 Section 4 *para* 1 Third Restitution Act provides: "Were moveable assets acquired at a public auction or in the context of execution or insolvency proceedings or in return for payment from an authorized trader or from persons to whom the owner him or herself had entrusted them for their use, for management or other purposes, then they are only considered withdrawn in the sense of section 1 *para* 1 [note: and must therefore be restituted] if the purchaser knew or had to know that the property had been withdrawn."

65 Section 367 Austrian General Civil Code states: "An ownership complaint does not lie against the *bona fide* possessor of moveable property when he proves that he has acquired the property either at a public auction, from a tradesman authorized to carry

of acquisition in the context of execution or insolvency proceedings "for practical reasons and reasons of equity."

Regarding the acquisition from a person of confidence, the modification in contrast to section 367 Austrian General Civil Code was that the good faith was intended to be excluded in the event of knowledge (or negligent non-knowledge) that the object was part of withdrawn assets, i.e. that when the object was acquired from a non-authorized person, mere good faith regarding ownership was not enough if the connection to withdrawn assets was known to the acquirer or at least recognizable with due care.[67]

The individual elements of section 4 *para* 1 Third Restitution Act will now be assessed with regard to the Munch painting. A moveable asset and an acquisition in return for remuneration are given. The prerequisites of an acquisition from a person of confidence and especially of good faith, however, are not fulfilled.

a. Carl Moll and Marie Eberstaller as 'Persons of Confidence' (Intermediary Agents) entrusted by Alma Mahler-Werfel?

A prerequisite for the denial of restitution under section 4 *para* 1 Third Restitution Act was that Carl Moll or Marie Eberstaller qualified as persons of confidence (intermediary agents) of the owner, i.e. as persons "to whom the owner himself had entrusted them for use, preservation or other purposes" (section 4 *para* 1 Third Restitution Act). The URC Vienna assumed that Carl Moll or Marie Eberstaller had been entrusted with the painting by Alma Mahler-Werfel. In reality Alma Mahler-Werfel had in 1937 entrusted the paintings to the Austrian Gallery, which in turn returned them to Carl Moll (after Alma Mahler-Werfel's escape). Strictly speaking, therefore, Moll was only 'a person of confidence of a person of confidence'.

Whether an entrusting in the sense of § 367 Austrian General Civil Code could be assumed in the case of such a chain of intermediary agents has been disputed for a long time[68] and is today accepted by the prevailing doctrine.[69] Yet, the possibility that an intermediary agent refers to the acquisi-

---

out such trade or by purchase from someone to whom the plaintiff himself had entrusted the property for use, custody or any other purpose. In these cases full ownership is acquired by the *bona fide* possessor and the former owner is entitled only to demand damages against those who are liable to him therefore."

66 Illustrating remarks on the government suggestion [*Regierungsvorlage*] of the Third Restitution Act; printed in Heller/Rauscher/Baumann, *Verwaltergesetz - Rückgabegesetz - Zweites und Drittes Rückstellungsgesetz* (Wien 1947), p. 147.

67 Cf the Commentary by Heller/Rauscher/Baumann, *Verwaltergesetz - Rückgabegesetz - Zweites und Drittes Rückstellungsgesetz*, p. 206.

68 This is denied, for instance, by Hans Neuburg, *Kommentar zu den Rückstellungsgesetzen* (Wien 1949) p. 40.

69 Cf Karl Spielbüchler in: Peter Rummel (ed.), *Kommentar zum ABGB*, 3rd edition (Wien 2000), Rz 9 zu § 367 ABGB.

tion from another intermediary agent to who he himself had entrusted the object, must be rejected, since in this hypothesis the agent refers to possession, the appearance of a right[70], which he had caused himself. An act of 'entrusting' with Alma Mahler-Werfel's consent can subsequently only be accepted if one assumes that she agreed to give the painting to Moll. The latter was expressly denied by her in the restitution trial and could only be deemed evident by the URC Vienna by deducing from the transfer of the villa in Breitenstein in the form of a donation or a trust, that Alma Mahler-Werfel had entrusted her *total assets*, which she had left behind, to Moll or Marie Eberstaller. This conclusion, however, is certainly not the only logical conclusion and, apart from that, contradicts general experience of life.

b. Good faith of the acquirer?

Even if one accepts the 'entrusting' (as the URC Vienna did), the good faith of the purchaser still has to be examined. When acquiring from a non-authorized person, the purchaser must in principle have been convinced of the seller's ownership according to the then and currently prevailing doctrine and jurisdiction.[71] Good faith with respect to the authorization to sell is only sufficient when purchasing from a business person entitled to carry out such business.[72] The investigations carried out in the trial showed that the Gallery of the 19th Century and its director, Professor Grimschitz, knew that Alma Mahler-Werfel was the owner of art works including the Munch painting. This means that the good faith only extended to Moll's or Maria Eberstaller's authorization to sell, which would not in itself be sufficient.

Apart from that, the intended or actual use of the proceeds for the house on the Semmering would also not have been sufficient to assume such authorization: Had Alma Mahler-Werfel not known about the concrete negotiations in 1940 nor agreed to them, the behaviour of Moll and his

---

70 To the ratio of the privileged acquisition from a person of confidence, compare for instance Helmut Koziol & Rudolf Welser, *Bürgerliches Recht I*, 12th edition (Wien 2002), p. 298. A re-acquisition in good faith by the non-authorized seller is inadmissible, too: Spielbüchler in Rummel, *Kommentar zum ABGB*, 3rd ed. (2000), Rz 12 zu § 367.

71 Cf Heinrich Klang in: Heinrich Klang, *Kommentar zum ABGB*, I/2, 1st edition (Wien 1931), p. 79; Armin Ehrenzweig, *System des österreichischen allgemeinen Privatrechts I/2*, 2nd edition (Wien 1957), p. 190; Franz Bydlinski, *Juristische Blätter* (1967), p. 355; Koziol/Welser, *Bürgerliches Recht I*, 12th ed. (2002) p. 296; OGH in GlUNF 6644 (from 1913); OGH in SZ 39/65 = JBl 1967, p. 202. Of different opinion, however, is Spielbüchler in: Rummel, *Kommentar zum ABGB*, 3rd ed. (2000), Rz 6 zu § 367 ABGB (with reference to Franz Zeiller, *Commentar II/1*, p. 136) as well as earlier jurisdiction.

72 See, however, Koziol/Welser, *Bürgerliches Recht I*, 12th ed. (2002), p. 296.

daughter Marie could only be qualified as an agency of necessity,[73] which cannot replace an authorization, as accurately described in the second RC ruling.[74] Did Grimschitz therefore assume the existence of an authorization only because he thought that the proceeds would be used in Alma Mahler-Werfel's interests,[75] without her having given a corresponding authorization? If so, he made an error concerning the law.

Account also has to be taken of good faith in terms of section 4 Third Restitution Act: This is reliant on the fact that the purchaser did not know (or did not have to know) that the property was that of a victim of National Socialism. The fact that Alma Mahler-Werfel had to be considered a victim of political persecution, however, was known to everybody involved. For this reason alone, the acceptance of an acquisition in good faith in accordance with section 4 *para* 1 Third Restitution Act is completely incomprehensible.

c. Independence of the acquisition from the National Socialist takeover of power?

Apart from that, a demand for return by Alma Mahler-Werfel would have by no means been impossible, even if there had been valid authorization. Even if Alma Mahler-Werfel had carried out the sale to the Gallery by herself, she could have claimed restitution as a victim of political persecution under the Third Restitution Act, unless it could be proved that the purchase would also have occurred irrespective of the National Socialists' takeover of power (section 2 *para* 1 Third Restitution Act).

This may have been the reason why the URC added in its verdict (despite accepting the requirements of section 4 Third Restitution Act) that "due to the above mentioned correspondence between Professor Moll and Dr Schwarz[76] ... it [can] quite safely be assumed to be evident that the sale of the painting would also have taken place irrespective of the takeover of power."[77]

---

73 In as far as they really wanted to act for Alma Mahler-Werfel, but not out of a personal interest in the repair and extension of the villa on the Semmering, which they used themselves.

74 Unless the proprietor [*Geschäftsherr*] later agrees.

75 As can be seen from, for example, the witness statement given by Dr Felicitas Hamburger, a close friend of Moll, at the request of the *Finanzprokuratur*: "He therefore decided to sell the Munch painting since he thought this would be in the applicant's interest ... I do not know anything about a written authorization." (witness statement on 25 September 1959, file pp. 161 - 162).

76 The URC here refers to letters of March 1938, in which Moll negotiates the sale of the Munch painting in Alma Mahler-Werfel's name. The authorization claimed by Moll was denied by Alma Mahler-Werfel in the restitution proceedings.

77 Rkb 186/53 = Rk 216/61, file p. 381.

This seems remarkable, especially because, according to the URC's jurisdiction regarding the Third Restitution Act, mere considerations to sell (even if made before 13 March 1938) were by no means sufficient to prove that the transaction was independent of the takeover of power by the National Socialists.[78] A crucial fact for the assumption of 'independence' was that the sale should take place under the *same or similar conditions* to those serving as the basis for negotiations before March 1938[79] and also that the sale should serve the *same economic purpose*[80]. Neither of these conditions applied in the case of the sale of the Munch painting: Alma Mahler-Werfel wanted to sell the beloved painting only in order to fund her escape, but not to fund the costs of repairing the roof of the house in Breitenstein during her enforced absence. She tried to sell the painting abroad herself so that she could obtain the possible proceeds herself; apart from that, there had been no further contact with her before the painting was sold to the Gallery.

The overall conclusion – irrespective of the URC's exceptionally[81] emotional appraisal, which was very unfavourable for the claimant – is therefore that the 1953 decision of the URC Vienna (even on the basis of the circumstances taken for granted by the URC) is in sharp contrast to the provisions of the Third Restitution Act and must consequently simply be qualified as unsustainable. In fact, compared to the general jurisdiction of the Restitution Commissions (which we studied extensively in the 'Practice of the Proceedings before the Restitution Commissions for the Historical Commission of the Republic of Austria' project[82]) the decision of the URC is a rare case that has to be viewed as a clear misjudgement.

The decision by Dr Ehrenzweig of the RC Vienna regarding the obligation to restitute the Munch painting, on the other hand, has to be viewed as completely in accordance with the legal provisions of the Third Restitution Act and the decisions of the Supreme Restitution Commission.

---

78 Cf SRC of 3 July 1948, Rkv 63/48 = Heller/Rauscher, *Die Rechtsprechung der Rückstellungskommissionen I* (1949) No.73; SRC of 19 June 1948, Rkv 83/48 = Heller/Rauscher, ibid., No.92. In general, transactions disposing over property caused by emigration were qualified as not "independent of the takeover of power"; compare, for instance, URC Vienna of 10 September 1948, Rkb 817/48 = Heller/Rauscher, ibid., No. 221.
79 SRC of 11 September 1948, Rkv 111/48 = Heller/Rauscher, ibid., No. 120
80 URC Vienna of 26 August 1948, Rkb 759/48 = Heller/Rauscher, ibid., No. 219.
81 As already discussed, the investigation of the circumstances and the appraisal of evidence of the first and second instance are diverging, with the URC's position being considerably less favourable for the applicant than the position of the RC.
82 Cf Meissel/Olechowski/Gnant, *Untersuchungen zur Praxis der Verfahren vor den Rückstellungskommissionen*, summarizing p. 395 ff.

C) The Mahler-Werfel restitution case as 'extreme injustice' in the sense of the General Settlement Fund Law 2001

The previous legal analysis was based on arguments that did not touch on the question of the legally binding effect of the Upper Restitution Commission's ruling. Nevertheless, the question arises as to whether a misjudgement – and in this case, an evident misjudgement – of the post-war era should still be considered eligible for restitution today.

Austrian legislation itself recently gave an answer to this question in the General Settlement Fund Law (BGBl I 2001/12), which was enacted in order to offer a "comprehensive solution for open questions regarding the compensation" of victims of National Socialism. This law makes clear that official decisions, but also restitution settlements (irrespective of their legally binding effect!) shall not be observed if the decision or settlement is considered "extremely unjust".[83] Despite all the ambiguity in the term 'extreme injustice', this term is at any rate taken to mean an extremely inaccurate application of legal provisions and one deemed to occur if proceedings in compliance with the law would have required a substantially different decision.[84] In accordance with the decision practice of the Arbitral Authority for Restitution in Kind, established in accordance with the General Settlement Fund Law,[85] the existence of an extreme injustice is to be assessed on the basis of a comparison with a "hypothetically correct" decision of the restitution authority,[86] and the question of whether the "legal foundations were inadmissibly interpreted and applied to the disadvantage of the damaged person"[87] in the particular case shall be examined.

In the case of the restitution of the Munch painting denied to Alma Mahler-Werfel this question has to be answered in the affirmative, given the inadmissibility of the reasoning in the legally binding decision of the URC Vienna discussed above.

Sure enough, according to section 1 *para* 2 sentence 2 General Settlement Fund Law, the special legal provisions for the restitution of art objects

---

83 Sections 10 *para* 1, 15 *para* 1 clause 2, 28 *para* 1 clause 2 and *para* 2 clause 2, as well as 32 *para* 2 clause 1 General Settlement Fund Law, BGBL I 2001/12.
84 Georg Graf, 'Arisierung und Restitution', *Juristische Blätter* (2001), p. 746 ff; Franz-Stefan Meissel, 'Unrechtsbewältigung durch Rechtsgeschichte?', *Juridikum* (2003), p. 42 ff; Walter H. Rechberger, 'Ist Ungerechtigkeit komparationsfähig?', *Juridikum* (2005), p. 59 ff.
85 Its members are Josef Aicher (Professor of commercial law at the University of Vienna) as chairman as well as August Reinisch (Associate Professor of Public International Law at the University of Vienna) and Erich Kussbach (a former Austrian career diplomat and honorary professor of Public International Law at the University of Linz).
86 Arbitral Authority for Restitution in Kind, decision number 27/2005, Rz 445 and 477.
87 Arbitral Authority for Restitution in Kind, decision number 3/2003, p. 20, 22; decision number 27/2005, Rz 444.

are still applicable. Although the provisions of the General Settlement Fund Law cannot be directly applied to the restitution in kind of art objects, the idea of coherence of values still requires the general sense of the legal values expressly stated in the General Settlement Fund Law for the application of the Art Restitution Act 1998 to be consulted for the purposes of legal analogy (in the sense of section 7 Austrian General Civil Code).

It cannot be claimed that the lawmaker imposes the criterion of extreme injustice for the correction of individual cases as far as the restitution in kind of real estate (in proceedings before the arbitral authority under the General Settlement Fund Law) is concerned, but not as far as valuations regarding the restitution of art works are concerned. This would represent an unobjective differentiation in contradiction with the principle of objectivity under Austrian constitutional law (article 7 Federal Constitution Law [B-VG]). However, in line with the generally accepted rule of systematic interpretation of the law, an interpretation in accordance with the constitution must be preferred. In other words, an interpretation that advances the unity of the legal order.[88]

In the opinion of the Supreme Court the legislative body that the General Settlement Fund Law lays down "must be understood now as good manners when solving compensation questions." In this respect its purpose as a legal signal extends beyond the immediate scope of regulation.[89] In this sense, the perspective of an extreme injustice in the sense of the General Settlement Fund Law should also be considered in respect of the question of restituting the Munch painting to the legal successors of Alma Mahler-Werfel.

This means that even if the URC's 1953 decision was binding with regard to the Munch painting in the context of the Art Restitution Act 1998 – and, for the above reasons, this is obviously not assumed in this legal opinion – it would still not be decisive for the question of a restitution obligation today according to section 1 clause 2 Art Restitution Act 1998, given the proven extreme injustice of the 1953 decision.

At last: The new Recommendation by the Advisory Board and Restitution of the Painting in May 2007

From a legal point of view, a new discussion of the issue by the Art Restitution Advisory Board was not excluded since the 1999 recommendation was not legally binding (see footnote 42 ff). Theoretically, the competent Federal Minister could even have effected restitution without a new (positive) recommendation by the Advisory Board since the Advisory

---

88 Cf. Franz Bydlinski, *Juristische Methodenlehre und Rechtsbegriff*, 2nd edition (Wien 1991), p. 455 ff.
89 OGH [Supreme Court] 30 September 2002, 1 Ob 149/02x = *Juristische Blätter* (2003), p. 454.

Board merely has the right to be heard and since – as elaborated above –our legal analysis demonstrates that the legal provisions for restitution under section 1 clause 2 Art Restitution Act 1998 were undoubtedly fulfilled in the case of the Munch painting. Thus Marina Mahler (represented by her Dutch lawyer, Gert-Jan van den Bergh) requested restitution of the painting in February 2006 for the second time. She based her claim on a legal expert opinion by the author of this paper, in which the above arguments were laid down.

Supported by a report from the new President (Werner Fürnsinn, a former Judge at the Austrian Supreme Court of Administrative Law) of the Commission of Provenance Research in Austrian Federal Museums, which recommended a new debate on the issue, the Art Restitution Advisory Board agreed to discuss Ms Mahler's request again at the session of June 2006. The Art Restitution Advisory Board, however, did not reach a decision immediately and postponed the matter to its autumn session, thus keeping matters hanging in suspense. In the meantime Marina Mahler's claim was confirmed by two other legal opinions issued by internationally renowned scholars (Ewald Wiederin, Professor of Public Law at the University of Salzburg and Paul Oberhammer, Professor of Civil Procedure at the University of Zurich). In its session of November 2006, the Advisory Board accepted the new arguments and (in a unanimous decision) advised the Minister to restitute the Munch painting.

Five months later, on 9 May 2007, Claudia Schmied, Austria's current Minister of Culture and Education, handed the Munch painting to Marina Mahler at a memorable ceremony in the Marble Hall of the Belvedere Museum. Seventy years after the loan to the museum, 67 years after the looting and 43 years after Alma's death, the Munch painting was finally returned to the family of Alma Mahler-Werfel. At last, justice prevailed.[90]

---

90 Translated by Irene Eckart and Franz-Stefan Meissel.

Who is a victim of Nazism?
West Germany and its approach to private participation in the Aryanization Policy during the Nazi Era

Jürgen LILLTEICHER[*]

"The execrable measures of spoliation and defamation of the National Socialist state against the Jews and other, in its eyes, unwanted creatures are celebrating their resurrection. This political legislation does not come to an end. Politics disguised as law, judicial decisions which heavily affect justice! This cannot just be overlooked by someone who thinks that justice is more than interpretation of laws – whoever has promulgated them – justice is a higher moral value. Laws are made by men. Someone who robbed in former times must not be robbed now. The people demand justice not only in a formal manner. It looks like the people do not trust the judicial authorities anymore. The moral consequences will be catastrophic."[1]

This was Alfred Steger's public comment on the restitution laws promulgated and implemented by the Allied Occupying Forces in West Germany after 1945. All property that had been stolen during the Nazi era had to be returned to the rightful owners. Steger was a member of the Federal Democratic Party and a member of the parliament of Rhineland-Palatinate, one of the German *Länder* re-established after the war. He was also a member of the Board of Executives of the 'Federal Association for Loyal Restitution'. This lobby organization was founded by private people who disputed their obligation to return property that they had seized or simply bought from persecuted German Jews during the Nazi era. Steger's comments were published in *Die Restitution*, the propaganda paper of this organization, on 30 April 1950.

---

[*] The following chapter is based on: J. Lillteicher, *Raub, Recht und Restitution. Die Rückerstattung jüdischen Eigentums in der frühen Bundesrepublik* (Göttingen 2007).

[1] "Das fluchwürdige Verfahren der Enteignung und der Diffamierung vom nationalsozialistischen Staat gegenüber den Juden und anderen in seinen Augen mißliebigen Kreaturen angewendet, feiert seine Auferstehung. Die politische Gesetzgebung nimmt kein Ende! Politik, die sich mit dem Recht tarnt, richterliche Entscheidungen, die die Gerechtigkeit schwer beeinträchtigen! Das alles kann einfach nicht übersehen werden, wer der Auffassung ist, daß Gerechtigkeit nicht nur durch Auslegung von Gesetzesparagraphen, mögen sie stammen von wem auch immer, sondern ein höchster sittlicher Wert ist. Auch Gesetze sind Menschwerk. [....] Wer damals nicht geraubt hat, darf jetzt nicht beraubt werden. Das Volk verlangt von seinen Machthabern Recht, und das nicht nur im formellen Sinne. Es sieht ganz danach aus, als ob die Justiz im Vertrauen des Volkes immer mehr genauso in die Kreide gerät wie die Gesetzgeber. Die moralischen Auswirkungen werden katastrophal sein." Alfred Steger, 'Restitution – aber loyal!', *Die Restitution* (30 April 1950), Vol. 1, p. 9 ff.

This speech can be described as a typical reaction by organized restitutors to the Allied restitution laws introduced in 1947 in the American and French zones and in 1949 in the British zone of occupation. The obligation of private people to return the property they gained during the National Socialist period was in most cases seen as an expropriation and a result of victors' justice.

The question I would like to answer in this article is: How could West Germany on the one hand go along with the guidelines of the Western Allied Military Governments and on the other hand deal with the turmoil caused by the above lobby organizations? The West German government faced massive resistance from restitutors or former aryanizers that endangered the stability of the West German post-fascist *Volksgemeinschaft*[2] in its process of transforming into a Western democratic society.

The debate on restitution was also a debate on different interpretations and representations of the Nazi past. A post-dictatorial community could only be stabilized by reaching a general consensus on the past. As the controversies over restitution dealt with the participation of individuals in the aryanization programme, the major issue was the relationship between the Nazi State and its citizens. How was consensus reached and did it change over time?

The 'Aryanization'[3] of Jewish property during the Nazi period in Germany was doubtless one of the most massive instances of property transfer in modern German history.[4] After 1945, the task of compensation posed a special challenge due to the fact that a large number of different parties participated in the non-uniform, almost anarchic process of dispossession and confiscation. The attempt to reverse the material consequences of that gigantic spree of plunder that later spread from Germany to the occupied territories and satellite states spawned a multitude of complex problems. On the one hand, there were limits to such a programme owing to the restricted judicial means available in a proper lawful procedure. On the other hand, property was to be restituted in a society whose members had been heavily implicated in National Socialist crimes of violence and 'Aryanization' before 1945.

Largely thanks to the Western Allies, particularly the Americans, a programme of restitution designed to do justice to the unusual character of the injustices perpetrated was ultimately implemented and rightfully pursued after the war. One consequence of Allied restitution legislation was that *all* legal transactions with Jews after 30 January 1933 were suspected of having

---

2 We cannot properly talk of a 'West German society' in the period immediately after the war. The Nazi *Volksgemeinschaft* had to be transformed into a democratic and open society with Western values. The term was coined by Lutz Niethammer.
3 See Frank Bajohr, *"Arisierung" in Hamburg: die Verdrängung der jüdischen Unternehmer 1933-1945* (Hamburg 1997), p. 9.
4 See Bajohr, *"Arisierung"*, p. 9.

been carried out under duress. This legislation also viewed all measures by the State and Nazi party that targeted the economic situation of Jews, ranging from discriminatory taxes and obligatory levies to the forced handing over of precious metals and other valuables, as unjustified 'dispossession'.[5]

Property transfers between Jews and non-Jews in Nazi Germany between 1933 and 1945 were checked on the basis of regulations that were mostly in accordance with German legal traditions. The Allied lawmakers consulted Jewish and non-Jewish German legal experts, who subsequently developed guidelines and clauses that could also be found in the *Bürgerliches Gesetzbuch* (German Civil Code). But the extraordinary injustice committed in the Nazi period could not wholly be dealt with in regulations established in the setting of nineteenth-century German society. Therefore new clauses unknown to German civil law had to be developed.[6] Later on it became clear that even these changes were not sufficient to deal with the theft policy of the Nazi State in occupied Europe. The theft of property in extermination camps had nothing to do with civil circumstances that could be catered for within the Civil Code.[7]

Three major regulations breaking with Germany's legal traditions were introduced into the restitution laws:

> a. A purchaser of Jewish property had to prove firstly that he had paid a fair price and secondly that the seller had had free access to that purchase price. For legal transactions after the announcement of the Nuremberg Laws in 1935, which was considered a major turning point in Nazi persecution policy towards the Jews in Germany, purchasers had to prove that the legal transaction would also have happened under normal circumstances, i.e. without the Nazis in power, and that they took account of the seller's interests.
>
> b. There was no protection for 'purchases in good faith'. The last owner had to return the property in question, regardless of whether he

---

5 'Deprival' (*Entziehung*) or 'dispossession' referred to the seizure or handover of property under duress. Since victims often found it impossible to prove there had been coercion, the law provided for facilitation of proof in the form of legal suspicion. The circumstances in which the court could accept that duress had been involved were determined, as were the conditions in which such suspicions could be refuted and rejected. See Walter Schwarz, *Die Rückerstattung der Alliierten Mächte* (München 1974), pp. 145-46.

6 After German reunification in 1989/1990 the Allied restitution programme was implemented in the Eastern part of Germany. This time restitution was embedded into German *Verwaltungsrecht* (administrative law).

7 For a detailed discussion of Federal Restitution Law and its implementation, see Jürgen Lillteicher, 'West Germany and the Restitution of Jewish Property in Europe', in: Martin Dean/Constantin Goschler/Philipp Ther (eds.), *Robbery and Restitution. The Conflict over Jewish Property in Europe* (New York 2007), pp. 99-112.

had known of the previous 'Aryanization'. As compensation for his loss he had a claim against the person or institution from whom or which he had bought the property. In several cases private persons bought or received Jewish property from the Nazi State. In this case, the person's claim was considered part of the overall debts of the German Reich, which in legal terms had gone bankrupt. Such a person's claim could only be dealt with after international agreement on the overall debt burden of the successor state.

c. Under German inheritance laws, heirless property would have fallen into the hands of the state. As whole families were killed and left no heirs, lawmakers wanted to prevent the successor state from inheriting property of Jews killed by the predecessor state and Nazi party organizations. The successor state was not allowed to profit from Nazi extermination policies. Jewish successor organizations were therefore set up and authorized to claim the heirless property in question.

It was this breach with German legal traditions and the underlying interpretation of the Nazi past that led to strong opposition from German politicians and anti-restitution activists. The idea that a person should be held responsible for his alleged participation in the persecution of German Jews was strongly rejected by politicians and citizens alike. In the Council of the *Länder* of the American zone of occupation in Stuttgart (*Stuttgarter Länderrat*) representatives initially objected to the idea of any form of private restitution.[8] After lengthy negotiations with the German representatives in the committee for property issues, the representatives agreed that at least Nazi profiteers would have to return property they gained through violence or massive pressure on the persecuted. With regard to some aspects, however, German opposition remained firm:

a. The judicial construction of an *Entziehungsvermutung* (an overall legal suspicion that handovers of property between 1933 and 1945 happened under duress). This *Entziehungsvermutung* had to be disproved by the purchaser in a certain manner, as explained above. The burden of proof was on the purchaser.

b. The breach with the protection of a 'purchase in good faith' provided for in the German Civil Code.

---

[8] The genesis of the restitution law in the American zone of occupation was analysed by Constantin Goschler, *Wiedergutmachung. Westdeutschland und di e Verfolgten des Nationalsozialismus, 1945-1954* (München 1992). The genesis of the restitution law in the British zone of occupation was examined in my study on restitution: J. Lillteicher, *Raub, Recht und Restitution. Die Rückerstattung jüdischen Eigentums in der frühen Bundesrepublik* (Göttingen 2007).

c. The establishment of Jewish Restitution Successor Organizations.[9]

It seemed that no harmony could be established between American restitution policy and the ideas discussed in the *Stuttgarter Länderrat* and the Allied Control Council. It is doubtful whether it was only the "impatience of the American Military Government[10]" – as Otto Küster, a German lawyer, representative in the *Länderrat* and, therefore, a biased contemporary witness, put it – that prevented Germans and Americans from reaching agreement on a common restitution law that would have been promulgated by the German authorities alone. On 11 November 1947 the American Military Government promulgated its own military law. On the same day, the French passed another decree on restitution for their occupation zone. This decree was strongly influenced by French legislation on restitution and allocated heirless Jewish assets to a fund to be used for paying compensation.[11] It was not until two years later, in May 1949, that the British military authorities decided[12] on legal regulations for restitution that, except for a few minor points, were identical to the American legislation.[13] After two years of restitution practice in the American zone the British were convinced that a restitution law could also be implemented in their zone of occupation without immense costs to British taxpayers.

The fact, however, that restitution laws were promulgated without German consent did not make the implementation of the restitution programme any easier. Those in Germany responsible for restitution regarded the law as an Allied dictate and a product of victors' justice. The trauma of Versailles, which resulted in any cooperation with the Allied powers being regarded as collaboration, was still virulent in the collective consciousness of judges and civil servants.[14]

---

9 The appointment of these organizations was also opposed by the French Military government. The French considered the Jewish Restitution Successor Organization to be a prolongation of Nazi racial categories in property law. Indeed it was difficult to decide after 1945 what was Jewish property: property of people who had been persecuted as Jews according to Nazi racial categories or people who were considered Jews under Jewish law?

10 Otto Küster, *Das geschäftliche Unternehmen in der Rückerstattung* (Heidelberg 1950), p. 55.

11 Decree No. 120 (10/11/1947) of the French commander in chief on the restitution of stolen assets, modified in decrees Nos. 156, 186 and 213. See *Journal Officiel du Commandement en Chef Francais en Allemagne* – official gazette of the French High Command in Germany 1949, Nos. 279, 280, 281 and 282, p. 2060.

12 The law took effect on 12/05/1949. *Amtsblatt der Militärregierung Deutschland* (official gazette of the German military government), Britisches Kontrollgebiet (British occupation zone), Nos. 28, p. 1169.

13 Although general decree No. 10 froze assets and made it possible to claim restitution early on, there was no generally binding legislation until 1949.

14 See, for instance, Schumacher's defaming of Adenauer as 'Chancellor of the Allied Powers.' See C. Goschler, 'Die Politik der Rückerstattung in Westdeutschland', in: C.

It was not only judges and officers in charge who had an uncomfortable feeling about Allied restitution laws. The restitutors themselves united in pressure groups such as *Verband der Rückerstattungsgeschädigten*, *Die Judengeschädigten* or *Bundesverband für loyale Restitution*. The names of these organizations showed that their members saw themselves as victims of restitution or even as damaged by Jews. By professional lobbying they flooded politicians in the *Länder* parliaments with petitions, while after the foundation of the new Federal Republic of Germany it was the members of the new *Deutsche Bundestag* (German parliament) that became their target. Through legal counselling and the publication of a periodical called *Die Restitution* ('The Restitution') the organizations sought to gain influence on restitutors and their legal strategies in restitution cases in German civil courts. Lobbyists spread hope among restitutors that, with the termination of the occupation statute, the Allied restitution programme would come to an end, and therefore restitutors should try to defer their cases until West Germany regained full sovereignty and control over the restitution programme. Another major demand was that those who had already returned property to former owners should be indemnified by the West German State. The comment by Alfred Steger at the start of this article was one example of their typical rhetoric. These organizations and its members found support within the Federal Democratic Party, which had already been infiltrated by former Nazis.

The Allies, in this case the Americans and the British, observed these activities very closely. The American High Commissioner, John J. McCloy, and the British High Commissioner, Ivone A. Kirkpatrick, publicly announced that the restitution programme would continue even after the occupation statute ended.[15]

Restitution and the Federal Republic of Germany

After the new Federal Republic of Germany was founded in 1949 private restitutors found strong supporters of their case within the first German government under Chancellor Konrad Adenauer. The Minister of Justice in Adenauer's cabinet, Thomas Dehler (FDP), pressed for standardization of the different restitution laws applying in the different zones of occupation. This standardization implied German control of the restitution process, i.e. that the *Bundesgerichtshof* ('Federal Court') would replace the Court of Restitution Appeals in the American zone, the Board of Review in the

---

Goschler & J. Lillteicher, *"Arisierung" und Restitution: Die Rückerstattung jüdischen Eigentums in Deutschland und Österreich nach 1945 und 1989* (Göttingen 2002), p. 110.

15 See I. A. Kirkpatrick to the Minister President of Lower Saxony, Hinrich Wilhelm Kopf, of 27.7.1951, Public Record Office Kew (PRO), FO 1008/82. Press Release No. 6884 12.6.1951, Archive of the Bavarian Ministry of Justice (BayJM) 1101a, Vol. 10.

British zone and the *Cour Supérieure pour les restitutions* in the French zone, while an indemnification programme would be set up for those restitutors who, in German eyes, had suffered injustices as a result of the Allied restitution laws.

On 4 November 1949 the Federal Democrats were the first to enter a petition in the *Deutsche Bundestag* demanding standardization and amendment of the existing restitution laws.[16] At this early stage, members of parliament feared that an open public debate on restitution in the German parliament would have an adverse effect on German-Allied relations. Therefore the matter was transferred to a parliamentary subcommittee in which all political parties were represented. This subcommittee would discuss all matters quite openly, but not in public view. It would be another year before West German MPs dared to comment publicly on Allied restitution laws and how they were implemented. Nevertheless discussions in the subcommittee continued. Further petitions followed. Members of the Bavarian Christian Social Union (CSU) filed a petition on 2 June 1950,[17] while the CDU/CSU also filed a petition on 10 October 1950,[18] two days after a public announcement by the American High Commissioner McCloy in which he stated that restitution would also continue after the occupation statute ended.[19] The strategy of Adenauer's government was twofold. Officially it agreed with the Allied guidelines in order to create a positive atmosphere in the important negotiations on the termination of the occupation statute, while Parliament and its subcommittees pressed forward with amendments of existing laws or at least with an indemnification programme for 'loyal restitutors'.[20]

What interpretation of the Nazi past and the policy of the Allies lay behind the idea to indemnify the restitutors? The arguments brought forward by the *Länder* and members of the *Bundestag* were the following.[21]

The Nazi regime as a whole persecuted specific groups who did not fit the Nazi ideology. Therefore the German people as a whole, rather than the

---

16 Cf. Kabinettsprotokolle 1951, Vol. 4, 1951, p. 122, Fn. 36. Deutscher Bundestag. Erste Wahlperiode 1949-1953, Drucksache No. 159, Antrag der Abgeordneten Nöll v.d. Nahmer betr. Vereinheitlichung des Rückerstattungsrechts, Anlagen, vol.1
17 Antrag der Abgeordneten Dr. Solleder, Dr. Horlbacher, Bauereisen und Genossen vom 2.6.1950, Deutscher Bundestag 1. Wahlperiode 1949, BDrs. No. 1010.
18 Cf. Deutscher Bundestag, 1. Wahlperiode 1949, Anfrage Nr. 125 der Fraktion der CDU/CSU, BT Drs. No. 1455
19 'Freiheit und Frieden nur durch gemeinsame Anstrengungen', *Neue Zeitung* (10 October 1950).
20 The term 'loyal restitutors' means people who have purchased in good faith and were ordered to return the property to its rightful owner.
21 Aktenvermerk zu Stellungnahme der Länder zur Frage einer Vereinheitlichung des Rückerstattungs- und Wiedergutmachungsrechts vom 6.4.1950, Anlage zum Schreiben von Dehler an den Staatssekretär des Innern im Bundeskanzleramt vom 1.5.1950, BArch, B 136/1124 Bl. 43–49; Cf. Stenographische Berichte des Deutschen Bundestages, 120. Sitting, 22.2.1951, pp. 4589–4599.

individual purchaser who bought an object in more or less good faith, were responsible for the consequences of this collective offence. As it was the State that provoked the actual obligation for restitution by its persecution policy it was the successor state that had to be held responsible for the consequences of this policy.

This interpretation of the past, which transferred responsibility for injustices from private people to the Nazi State, had its limits. The successor state would never accept an enforceable legal claim for compensation. Those who returned property to the rightful owners in situations where the State had actually been the spoliator should be entitled to receive compensation, which would be estimated according to the distributive principles of the welfare state and, therefore, according to the principles of the common equality of burdens (*Lastenausgleich*).[22] The self-proclaimed *Rückerstattungsgeschädigten* ('victims of restitution') would never be compensated for their actual loss; instead the compensation would be measured according to the scope available within the budget of the new federal state.

The competition between these corrective and distributive principles of justice was and still is a central issue in the history of restitution. The outcome of the debate on damages caused by the Allied restitution programme after 1945 was also crucial for the victims of Nazi persecution before 1945. Any compensation paid to restitutors would have to be paid out of the overall budget reserved for restitution claims by dispossessed original owners against the former German Reich. As these debts were considered part of the overall German debts on which no international agreement had been reached at that time, it had to be decided whether debts deriving from restitution should be excluded from the solution of the overall debt question and paid in advance.

If the self-proclaimed *Rückerstattungsgeschädigten* were to be compensated, a payment in advance had to be made. Of course this idea encountered strong opposition from the Ministry of Finance, which considered these debts to be part of the overall problem of German pre-war and post-war debts. Leading officials at the Ministry of Finance believed that the reduced territory of West Germany in comparison to the territory of Germany in 1937 and the resulting reduced tax revenues of the West German Treasury should be taken into account when the maximum amount paid under the Allied restitution programme was negotiated.[23]

---

22 The *Lastenausgleich* programme was enacted in order to spread the consequences of war equally manner. For example, German expellees received money from this programme, while others, who had suffered less, had to pay special levies in addition to their taxes.
23 *Ministerialrat* Friedrich Kuschnitzky in his speech to the German *Bundestag*. Kurzprotokoll der 100. Sitzung des Ausschusses für Rechtswesen und Verfassungsrecht vom 25.4.1951, BArch, B 136/1124. Bl. 216.

The remarkable aspect of this debate was that the quarrel about compensation for restitutors accelerated the search for a solution to the restitution claims of Jews against the former German Reich, in particular restitution for the payment of discriminatory taxes and levies such as the *Reichsfluchtsteuer* and *Judenvermögensabgabe*. As the restitutors – in contrast to the victims of Nazi persecution – were potential voters, their interests had a bigger lobby than those of the victims. The result was a package deal, which was typical of the Adenauer government's *Vergangenheitspolitik*.

The fates of the victims and those of the restitutors were consequently connected to the general question of German debts. But what were the conditions for compensation or what cases of so-called 'unjust restitution' should be compensated? The following cases can be considered as hardship suffered by private restitutors:

a. One of the questions that had to be answered during a restitution trial was whether the purchase price had been at the free disposal of the persecuted person. If the State intervention had caused payment of an unfair purchase price, which was then transferred to a blocked bank account, the purchaser was held partly responsible for the State's actions and therefore had to return the property to the rightful owner and would not receive compensation from the successor state. Private people were held partly responsible for the intervention of the Nazi State as they had taken advantage of its persecution policy.

b. The current possessor of the property in question had to return the property regardless of whether he was the person who originally bought the property from a persecuted person. In exchange, the restitutor could file a claim against the person who originally sold the Jewish property to him. If both the seller and confiscator were the Nazi State, the restitutor and actual possessor would not be able to enforce his claim against the German Treasury until international agreement on overall German debts had been reached.

The question of who was authorised to receive compensation for restitution caused severe controversies in the German *Bundestag* in the 1950s and 1960s. It was difficult to differentiate between those who obtained property through connections to Nazi Party officials and those who had honestly not known about the preceding property transactions. The *Gauwirtschaftsberater* could forbid certain property transactions, while the *Reichsstatthalter* and *Gauleiter* of certain cities initiated 'Aryanizations' in favour of Party members in exchange for *Arisierungsspenden* ('Aryanization donations') for the Nazi Party Treasury.[24]

---

24 The *Gauleiter* of Hamburg, Karl Kaufmann, developed a refined system of using the Aryanization policy for the financial wellbeing of the Hamburg Nazi Party. See Frank

To what extent could private individuals be held responsible for their participation in Nazi persecution policy? Political activists such as Alfred Steger obviously tried to summarize almost all property transactions as 'loyal purchases or purchases in good faith' and claimed an enforceable right of compensation. Politicians, especially from the Social Democratic Party, were well aware of this strategy. During the debates, Social Democratic MPs in particular stressed that no "*braunen Aasgeier*"[25] ('brown vultures') should receive compensation. Carlo Schmid in particular criticised the rhetoric of the activists in which "also former SS and SD members start to consider themselves victims of National Socialism."[26] This was a strong argument against a wide interpretation of the term 'victim of the Nazi period'.

Although influential politicians such as Otto Küster, a lawyer and state secretary for restitution issues in Württemberg-Baden, supported the cause of those who suffered hardship as a result of Allied restitution measures, they never accepted an overall claim for compensation.

The impression from the various debates initiated by petitions in the German *Bundestag* is that the Allied restitution laws were considered a cause of severe injustices and that restitutors had to be compensated, particularly if the different restitution laws in the Allied zones of occupation could not be unified in a Federal Restitution Law under German control. The Federal State, which lacked power in restitution matters due to the Allied rights of reservation und the occupation statute, had to find ways of demonstrating sovereignty to certain lobby groups by establishing a compensation scheme.

The discussions about the ending of the occupation statute in 1952 resulted in an international treaty (*Überleitungsvertrag*)[27] in which the Federal Government guaranteed that the Allied restitution laws would remain in effect after the Allies handed over sovereignty to the Germans. In exchange, the payment of restitution claims against the German Reich was limited to a total of 1.5 billion Deutschmarks, while two German judges were appointed to join the Supreme Restitution Court under a neutral chairman.

The negotiations also revealed a certain impression that Adenauer had of the attitudes prevailing among members of the German *Bundestag* and

---

Bajohr, *Parvenus und Profiteure. Korruption in der NS-Zeit* (Frankfurt am Main 2001), and Frank Bajohr, *"Arisierung" in Hamburg. Die Verdrängung der jüdischen Unternehmer 1933-45* (Hamburg 1997).

25 See: Die SPD-Abgeordneten Greve und Schmid, Stenographische Berichte des Deutschen Bundestages, 120. Sitzung, 22.2.1951, pp. 4589 - 4599
26 Idem.
27 Vertrag zur Regelung aus Krieg und Besatzung entstandener Fragen oder kurz Überleitungsvertrag, abgedruckt in: *Verträge der Bundesrepublik*, Serie A: Multilaterale Verträge, Auswärtiges Amt, Vol. 7 (Bonn/Cologne/Berlin 1957), pp. 223–279 (trilingual).

within German society in general. A restitution process solely under Allied control and without a certain limit to restitution claims against the German Reich would trigger severe anti-Semitism in German society, while the German *Bundestag* would never approve a treaty with such contents. On the one hand the negotiations in the German *Bundestag* revealed that Adenauer was right in his diagnosis that latent anti-Semitism could be made manifest, but on the other hand Adenauer deliberately used German anti-Semitism as a weapon in negotiations with the Allies in order to reduce the overall restitution debts. There was nothing the Allies feared more than disturbances among the German public and manifestation of latent anti-Semitism. This scenery of threat built up by Adenauer was not taken seriously by representatives of Jewish organizations. After a request for comment by the American State Department the Republican Member of Congress Jakob Koppel Javits – a leading representative of Jewish interests in Congress – said that he would take the risk of anti-Semitism. Nahum Goldmann, chairman of the World Jewish Congress, and Jakob Blaustein, Chairman of the American Jewish Committee (AJC), came up with similar answers. They answered laconically that, in Germany, you had to reckon with a certain amount of anti-Semitism anyway.[28] Jewish organizations would not accept the rhetoric of German politicians and accepted the risk of manifest anti-Semitism, which was not the responsibility of the Jewish organizations but of West German society.

As an indemnification programme for restitutors was not enforceable against the will of the Allies the West German government had to find other ways of satisfying the pressure groups. On 20 May 1960 the Adenauer government decided in favour of compensation for restitutors.[29] Before these regulations came into force, restitutors could write off their restitution obligations in their annual tax returns. They could amortize their financial losses as the finance authorities accepted their petition for lower income and corporation taxes.[30] The procedures for a state tax credit used different criteria to assess the Aryanization of Jewish property than those established in the restitution laws. At least some parts of the German Civil Code that had been abandoned by the Allies were applied to the Aryanization and the results of restitution.

An official programme of compensation for restitution was integrated into the *Reparationsschädengesetz* ('RepG') (Law on Damages caused by Reparations, Restitution, Destruction and Internal Restitution) of February

---

28 See Oliver Franks, British Embassy, to Anthony Eden, Foreign Office, of 23.1.1952, PRO, FO 371/97793. See Goschler, *Wiedergutmachung*, p. 252 ff.
29 See Allgemeines Kriegsfolgengesetz (AKG) vom 5. November 1957 See BGBl. I, 1957, p. 1747.
30 See Féaux de la Croix an den Bundesfinanzminister vom 28.2.1957, BArch, B 126/42630.

1969.³¹ This law provided compensation specifically for purchasers who had paid a fair purchase price that was confiscated by the State and, therefore, not at the free disposal of the persecuted person. Interestingly enough lobbyists such as Alfred Steger tried to hide their original interests behind those who lost their property in Allied countries during the war, including large international companies such as I.G. Farben. Speakers, such as Martin Hirsch from the Social Democrats, who were more critical about the compensation claims, provided a more balanced analysis of private participation in Nazi injustices. Social Democrats had also been persecuted and had suffered severe property losses. As he said in the *Bundestag* debate on 20 February 1960:

> "It is my opinion that someone who bought property of politically and racially persecuted persons acted at his own risk. He knew that person was a Jew, he knew that person was a Social Democrat, he knew that this company was owned by the Zentrum Party, or the leftist youth movement. He knew or should have known about it. It is a fact that in nearly all cases the seller would not have sold his property if he had not been under severe pressure of political and racial persecution. It is therefore clear that these Aryanizations or property transfers from persecuted people to non-persecuted people were never loyal [...]. In recent months we have been flooded by petitions. If you are an expert in the field of restitution and you read all these petitions you will recognize that most of these writers are on the wrong path, pushed by men behind them. The petitioners are sort of frontrunners for those who have bigger interests but who do not need the money. The latter are running behind them and they just want to feather their own nests.³²"

---

31 See Gesetz zur Abgeltung von Reparations-, Restitutions-, Zerstörungs- und Rückerstattungsschäden (Reparationsschädengesetz–RepG) vom 12.2.1969, BGBl. I, 1969, pp. 105–136.

32 "Ich bin der Meinung, dass jemand, der Eigentum eines rassisch oder politisch Verfolgten erworben hat, auf eigenes Risiko gehandelt hat. Er wusste: das ist ein Jude; er wusste: das ist ein Sozialdemokrat; er wusste: das ist ein Unternehmen des Zentrums, der Deutschen Jugendkraft oder wer da alles in Betracht kam. Er hat gewusst oder hätte wissen müssen. Es steht fest, dass so gut wie in allen Fällen der Verkäufer nicht veräußert hätte, wenn er nicht unter einem rassischen oder politischen Druck gestanden hätte. Es besteht daher für mich die Vermutung, dass eine solche Arisierung oder ein solcher Erwerb von einem politisch oder rassisch Verfolgten an sich nicht loyal gewesen ist [...]. Wir sind in den letzten Monaten und Jahren alle mit Briefen von Rückerstattungsgeschädigten, Reparationsgeschädigten usw. überschüttet worden. In letzter Zeit war es eine Flut. Schaut man sich die Briefe an und versteht man was von den Dingen, muss man doch feststellen, dass das im allgemeinen irregeleitete Leute sind, die von irgendwelchen Hintermännern geschoben werden. [...] Sie sollen aber den Vorläufer spielen für Große, die das Geld nicht brauchen, die hinter ihnen her marschieren und ihre Schäfchen ins Trockene bringen wollen." Stenographische Berichte des Deutschen Bundestages, 4. Wahlperiode, 116. Sitzung vom 20.2.1964, pp. 5325–5326.

According to the RepG, 113,001 claims were filed. Of these, 81,059 petitions were successful, but the sums paid out totalled only 600 million Deutschmarks.[33] This showed that estimations by the Ministry of Finance, which had reckoned on 1.9 billion Deutschmarks (around 9.5 billion euros in today's money) for losses resulting from restitution alone, were inflated.[34] The general perception that the Allied restitution programme was the result of victors' justice and that most of the Aryanizations were correct and legal property transfers, was proved false by the results of the compensation paid. A review of the restitution courts' decisions, based on legal principles of the German Civil Code, revealed that most restitutors had not suffered injustice to the extent that the 'damaged by restitution' associations had claimed over and over again. Most of the petitions for compensation were rejected because the purchaser had not even paid a fair market price (90% of the market price). In other words, the basic requirements for a fair deal were not fulfilled.

Nevertheless the perception that the State was responsible for private profiteering from the Nazi persecution policy persisted from the 1940s – firstly in the *Stuttgarter Länderrat* – throughout the 1950s and until the late 1960s.

Restitutors have made a special sacrifice for Germany, which was compensated in the same way as the losses suffered by non-Jewish Germans displaced from Silesia or other German victims of the Second World War. The fact that the German *Bundestag* agreed in 1964 on a compensation model that went no further than the principle of the common equality of burdens showed that the self-proclaimed 'victims of restitution' should not be treated differently from the victims of the Nazis. It also highlighted the continuing sense of discomfort about the Allied restitution programme and its implicit interpretation of the Nazi past in West German society. The competition between an enforceable legal right for compensation and the principles of the welfare state, i.e. the competition between principles of corrective justice and distributive justice,[35] was decided in favour of the German Ministry of Finance's policy based on principles of distributive justice. In other words, denying any enforceable legal claim for compensation. In this case, the victims of the Holocaust and the German self-proclaimed 'victims of restitution' were dealt with in the same manner. The alternative would have been a compensation law that would have reversed the actual meaning and importance of the restitution programme.

---

33 Statistik für den Lastenausgleich, Statistischer Bericht LA – 4/2000, Statistik über die Durchführung des Reparationsschädengesetzes (RepG), Stand 31.12.1999, p. 1.
34 Bundestagsdrucksache V/2432, p. 77 ff.
35 For a discussion about these legal principles in the Dutch history of restitution, see: Wouter Veraart, *Ontrechting en rechtsherstel in Nederland en Frankrijk in de jaren van bezetting en wederopbouw* (Deventer 2005), pp. 32-46.

The fact that Aryanization and the question of participation in the National Socialist regime did not become a topic of open discussion and in-depth research in Germany until the 1990s is a result of the *Vergangenheitspolitik* of the Adenauer era and thereafter. West Germany made concessions to the Allies for which there was no real consensus in West German society. In exchange, the young republic was granted greater rights of sovereignty. Through solidarity statements in the German *Bundestag* and compensation the young state made it clear that private restitution was in many cases a sacrifice that private people made in situations where the State should have stepped in. Although restitutors did not get their total damage compensated, they could consider themselves to be people to whom no injustice had been done. The State used instruments of credit and tax privileges as a means of preventing further turmoil that could have caused people to drift away from the young democracy and back into ideological radicalism. After a time, the seal of silence was broken, once questions about private participation in Nazi injustices could openly be discussed without causing social instability. West Germany managed to create a 'passage of time' during which it could stabilize itself and develop from a post-Nazi *Volksgemeinschaft* into a liberal, democratic society.

Consequences of persecution
Antwerp as an example of restitution in Belgium (1944-1960) in comparative perspective with the Netherlands

Veerle VANDEN DAELEN (Antwerp)[*]

At a certain point in the Second World War the German occupier declared Antwerp *Judenrein*. During the occupation, more Jews fell victim to persecution and annihilation in Antwerp than in any other Belgian city, partly due to the negligent attitude of the local authorities. On their return after the liberation, Jews were confronted with the fact that their homes were occupied by other people and that their household effects had gone. The situation of the Jews was harrowing. There was a lack of resources and people to take care of the severely traumatised Jews and the new wave of refugees. It was very difficult to provide them with basic material needs such as food, shelter and clothing. Furthermore, these victims were mentally totally bewildered: they were uncertain about the fate of family and friends and were traumatised by the camps or by having had to go into hiding. Witnesses who visited Belgium in the year it was liberated describe pitiful circumstances. Approximately 80% of the Jews in Belgium had no furniture or clothes to call their own.[1] Nevertheless, Jewish life started getting back on its feet in the very first year after liberation.[2]

This chapter focuses on how the practical and legal consequences of the war were settled for Jews in Belgium, using Antwerp as an example, even though differences in the extent of persecution between cities created different living conditions for Jews in the various Belgian cities. The two cities with the largest Jewish populations in Belgium, Brussels and Antwerp, show differences in the presence of official Jewish structures at the end of the liberation and in the number of Jews deported from these cities. A total of 9,009 of the 13,779 Jews (65%) who were registered in Antwerp in March 1942 by the *Vereeniging van Joden in België* (VJB) (Association of Jews in Belgium) – an organization established by the Germans – had been transported to Auschwitz from the Dossin Barracks in Mechelen. If we look at other cities in Belgium with relatively large Jewish populations, we find that in Greater Liège, Greater Brussels and Greater Charleroi 35%,

---

[*] I would like to thank Prof. Dr. Herman Van Goethem (University of Antwerp) for his much appreciated help with juridical and legislative issues.
[1] American Jewish Archives ('AJA', Cincinnati), World Jewish Congress files ('WJC files'), D78/15, Belgium, children, Jan-Sept 1945, Report on the situation of the Jewish population in Belgium [several months prior to 27.6.1945].
[2] For more information on Antwerp during the first year after the liberation, see: V. Vanden Daelen, 'Returning: Jewish life in Antwerp in the aftermath of the Second World War (1944-1945)', *European Judaism* 38/2 (Autumn 2005), pp. 26-42.

37% and 38% respectively of the Jews registered by the VJB had been transported. In other words, the Jews of Antwerp were hit proportionally very hard. Just like Amsterdam, for example, Antwerp had been left by the German occupying forces as *Judenrein*: officially there was no Jewish life left. On German orders, Jewish societies had been dissolved and Jewish places of worship had been closed. The few Jews still in the city lived in hiding. In Brussels, on the other hand, some official Jewish organizations remained operative until the liberation.[3]

To put the Belgian situation into a wider perspective I will draw functional comparisons to the situation in the Netherlands. How similar or different was it to return as a Jew to Belgium than to the Netherlands? Due to the exceptional nature of German measures during the occupation, returning Jews were obliged once again to make themselves known as Jews after the liberation, this time in order to undo the consequences of the Nazi policies. This was the case both for those who chose to live a consciously Jewish life and for those who did not wish to assert themselves as Jews after the war. How heavy was the burden of the consequences of the wartime persecution?

This contribution will focus only on the possible restitution of assets of survivors or their legal heirs, not on what happened to the assets of whole families who died in the camps. The focus will be on movable and immovable property and will disregard insurance policies, businesses and art spoliation. I will focus on the first fifteen years after the war, from the liberation in 1944-1945[4] until 1960. The struggle with all the practical problems caused by the persecution and despoliation during the war, and the fact that often no solution was possible or offered, certainly influenced the outlook and development of post-war Jewish life in both the Netherlands and Belgium. As we see in the first few years after the war in the Netherlands, the disappointments experienced led to a difficult re-integration and high demand for emigration visas. Belgian research into the return of Jews after the war started only a couple of years ago, whereas in the Netherlands the post-war period has been the subject of substantial historical research. From that research it appears on the one hand that the trauma created by the Jews' reception and treatment by the Dutch authorities, who were criticized for excessive formalism, was enormous, and on the other hand that anti-Semi-

---

3 L. Saerens, *Vreemdelingen in een wereldstad. Een geschiedenis van Antwerpen en zijn Joodse bevolking (1880-1944)* (Tielt 2000), pp. 647-648; L. Saerens, 'Dossier Brussel en de joodse kwestie. Inleiding', *Bijdragen tot de Eigentijdse Geschiedenis* 12 (2003), p. 131; L. Saerens, 'Die Hilfe für Juden in Belgien', in: J. Benz and W. Wetzel (eds.), *Solidarität und Hilfe für Juden während der NS-Zeit, Regionalstudien 4: Slowakei, Bulgarien, Serbien, Kroatien mit Bosnien und Herzegowina, Belgien, Italien* (Berlin 2004), pp. 193-280.

4 Brussels was liberated by the Allied forces on 3 September 1944 and Antwerp on 4 September. Part of the neighbouring Netherlands followed soon afterwards, although other parts remained occupied until the German surrender on 5 May 1945.

tism was still very much alive after the liberation.[5] This chapter also examines how a country deals with its past and how this is reflected in its study of the past.

Despoliation

From the very start of the occupation, the intention of the anti-Jewish measures that were issued by the German *Militärverwaltung* (Military Administration) was to systematically identify, isolate and rob the Jews. Jewish real estate was seized, rented properties were allocated to new people and movable furniture was taken away as part of the *Möbelaktion* (furniture campaign) and transported to Germany.[6]

Democratic constitutional states had only very weak instruments at their disposal to rectify the dictatorial measures of the occupying forces. The legal systems of these states were unprepared to react adequately to the consequences of the occupier's policy of isolating one segment of the population. The actions of the Belgian government evidence this very clearly. Already during the war the Belgian government-in-exile in London, presided over by Prime Minister Pierlot, tried to take action. One of the first measures it took was the legal decree of 10 January 1941 regarding "the measures imposed by the enemy concerning deprivation of property."[7] This decree prescribed that all acts of disposition regarding movable and immovable property – confiscation, sequestration, forced sale "or all other measures that are an infringement on private property" – committed by the occupier from 10 May 1940 onwards were invalid *ab initio*. The injured party had the right to claim such property for up to three years after the start of the peace.

After the liberation it became very quickly apparent that measures such as the legal decree of 10 January 1941 contained loopholes. Indeed, the notion of 'forced' posed a problem. If a property had been handed over on German command the case was very clear, but more often than not the pressure to hand over a property had been indirect. For example, cases of Germans or collaborators approaching Jewish owner with proposals to sell their property for a set price were legion. It was suggested to the Jewish owners

---

5   M. Citroen, *U wordt door niemand verwacht. Nederlandse joden na kampen en onderduik* (Utrecht 1999); D. Hondius, *Terugkeer. Antisemitisme in Nederland rond de bevrijding* (The Hague 1990).
6   R. van Doorslaer (ed.), *De bezittingen van de slachtoffers van de jodenvervolging in België: Spoliatie – Rechtsherstel – Bevindingen van de Studiecommissie. Eindverslag van de Studiecommissie betreffende het lot van de bezittingen van de leden van de joodse gemeenschap van België, geplunderd of achtergelaten tijdens de oorlog 1940-1945* (Brussels 2001), pp. 39, 156.
7   Besluitwet van 10 januari 1941 inzake de door den vijand genomen maatregelen houdende ontheffing uit het bezit, *Belgisch Staatsblad* (London), 25 February 1941. (Translated from Dutch).

that they would avoid trouble this way, thus leading them to 'agree' to the (coerced) sale of their property. Other loopholes included the German decrees that gave Jews a set period of time to sell their property, after which, if the property had not been sold, a forced sale would be imposed.[8] As a result Jews experienced difficulties in restoring their property rights in almost every domain.

The Dutch government-in-exile also prepared measures for after the liberation to declare Nazi laws void and to restore the *status ante quo*. A legal decree of 7 June 1940 prohibited any legal actions, including economic transactions, between Dutch persons, firms, associations and so on with 'enemy citizens'. Very often, Jewish victims had literally been robbed, but this legal decree, referred to as 'A6', could offer no help in cases of theft. Nor was any satisfaction available to victims under Decree E100 on the restoration of legal relations, which came into being in September 1944 and was later amended by Decree F272.[9] There was, for example, an exception that allowed someone who had purchased assets in good faith to receive compensation from the original owner reclaiming his property, and this even applied to immovable property. After the liberation a Council for the Restoration of Rights (*De Raad voor het Rechtsherstel*) was established on 9 August 1945. With the exception of one department, which continued operating for longer, the Council remained in existence until 1 June 1967. Nevertheless the process of recovering rights was very arduous.[10]

Recovery of immovable property

Jews in the Netherlands did not receive any preferential treatment in the post-liberation assignment of housing. Michal Citroen registered the testimonies of returning Jews who were disappointed by the lack of help the Dutch authorities gave them to return to their homes or to find new accommodation.[11]

We do not have so many testimonies recorded in Belgium. However, just like in the Netherlands, Antwerp faced a huge housing shortage after the war.[12] The city had been a main target of massive German bombardments, and from 13 October 1944 until 29 March 1945 the city was under

---

8   AJA, WJC-files, H58/10, Belgium, Belgium Jewish Representative Committee, minutes, 1940-1945, Note, 30.4.1942.
9   The letters A, E and F stand for the year in which these decrees were passed (A is 1940, B 1941, C 1942, D 1943, E 1944, F 1945). It was a decision by the Dutch government-in-exile to clearly mark the decrees issued by the acting government until such time as the Second Chamber could function in a regular way (see G. Aalders, *Berooid: De beroofde joden en het Nederlandse restitutiebeleid sinds 1945,* (Amsterdam 2001), p. 40).
10 Aalders, *Berooid*, pp. 14, 32, 46, 52-53, 147.
11 Citroen, *U wordt door niemand verwacht*, pp. 104-105.
12 Ibidem.

fire on an almost daily basis. V-bombs killed thousands of people and caused considerable material damage.[13] Nevertheless, the recovery of homes in Belgium seems not to have posed any serious problems. The Allied forces even seem to have been very helpful to the returning Jewish population. Immediately after the liberation of Antwerp, for example, posters were affixed to certain houses stating: 'Reserved for Jewish refugees from [...] onwards'. This was probably the work of the Committee for the Defence of Jewish Interests (*Comité ter Verdediging van de Joodsche Belangen,* CVJB), whose leader, Jozef Sterngold, had officially been appointed by the Allied town mayor to take care of returning Jews.[14] The public prosecutor of Antwerp, Armand De Schepper, also issued an order immediately after the liberation prescribing the restitution to Jews of their homes as soon as possible.[15] Already on 8 September 1944 the chief superintendent of the Antwerp police wrote in his routine orders that the public prosecutor had informed him that in several areas of the city Jews wished to occupy their previous abodes, that on the prosecutor's orders the local police had to assist these people, that the current occupants of these abodes had to be advised to leave as soon as possible and that the matter needed to be dealt with in a tactful manner with the help of the police.[16]

From the above one could easily conclude that the recovery of the original residences in Antwerp would proceed smoothly and serenely. However there was one thing that had not been taken into account: the British military government. Even though the town mayor, Finch, was said to have appointed the Jewish resistance leader Josef Sterngold to organise the reception of returning Jews, some of these residences were still assigned a different use. Barely two days later Finch declared that all houses that had been occupied by German servicemen during the German occupation would

---

13 4,229 people were killed, 6,993 were wounded. These are the numbers believed to be correct today. Contemporary sources mention 2,300 dead or missing. The town mayor Camille Huysmans referred to 3,000 civilian victims and 3,000 soldiers in his speech on 5 February 1946 at the inauguration of a commemorative plaque to mark the bombardments. In addition there were more than 6,000 wounded. See 'V-bommen op Antwerpen. De dood valt uit de hemel', *Knack* (2004), pp. 52-56, based on: K. Palinckx, *Antwerpen onder de V-bommen, 1944-1945* (Antwerp 2004); United States National Archives (Washington), Record Group 84, Belgian Embassy, Memorandum for the United States Government, 23.1.1945; American Consulate General, Antwerp, to Secretary of State, Washington, Presentation of a Plaque to the City of Antwerp by Supreme Headquarters, Allied Expeditionary Forces, report of 12.2.1946).
14 Citroen, *U wordt door niemand verwacht,* p. 141.
15 Armand De Schepper was public prosecutor for the Antwerp District from January 25th, 1922 until December 19th, 1945. In August 1941 he was suspended by the German occupier, who thereby called upon the German decree of March 7th, 1941 that limited the age of public prosecutors to 60 years. Presumably De Schepper resumed his position after the liberation. See C. Laenens, *De geschiedenis van het Antwerps Gerecht* (Antwerp 1953), p. 648; Saerens, *Vreemdelingen in een wereldstad,* p. 495.
16 Stadsarchief Antwerpen, Politiearchief, Bevrijding, MA 41 747/20.1.

be occupied by British servicemen, even if the properties were the properties or residences of returned Jewish refugees.[17] The Jewish refugees were asked to turn to the Attaché for Civil Matters of the Allied Armies at Koningin Elisabethlaan 8 to have new housing assigned to them. The posters stating 'Reserved for Jewish refugees from [...] onwards' had to be removed.

However, if people owned a house in Belgium, it seems to have been reasonably easy for them to get it back within a short space of time.[18] There is very little published jurisdiction regarding the recovery of real estate, and this may be an indication of the lack of lawsuits and that it was relatively easy to recover property. Of course, claimants had to produce proof that they were indeed the actual owners of the property. If owners had died, people claiming the property had to prove that they were the legal heirs of the deceased owners. If the owner was presumed to have died in a concentration camp, the case was postponed until after the official registration of death. Under the Royal Decree of 14 February 1946 and the law of 20 August 1948 a court had to pronounce the person in question to be presumably deceased.[19]

In Belgium these declarations to pronounce a person presumably deceased came much earlier than in the Netherlands, where claimants had to wait until at least 1949 in order to resolve inheritance problems relating to concentration camp victims. The Dutch government did not wish to make exceptional rules for Jewish victims, and so inheritance was granted only after the name of the deceased person had been entered into the city register of deaths. This caused many administrative problems, including the fact that the inheritance legislation needed information on which members of a family died first in order to decide who was the legal heir of an asset. And given

---

17 Stadsarchief Antwerpen, Politiearchief, Bevrijding, MA 41 747/20.2. The same thing happened in Brussels, where approximately 1,645 of the houses and premises that had been confiscated by the German occupier were recovered by the Allied forces (Le problème des biens sans maître, *Ofipresse*, 24 (19/10/1945), pp. 3-4).

18 On 16 September 1944 the Court of the First Instance of Antwerp assigned the lawyers Marck, Boelens and Van Put to manage the former German *Verwaltung* that had been under the command of the four *Verwalters* Hütteman, Voigt, Wauters and Wäser. This was a unique situation. After the liberation of other Belgian cities, Jewish immovable property fell under the command of the *Dienst van het Sekwester* (Department of Sequestration), established on 4 September 1944. A few at a time, Jewish owners returned and could claim back their properties if they could prove ownership. However, we have little or no information on the actual progress of the recovery of immovable properties in Antwerp, partly due to the lack of archives left by the post-war managers. Apparently the original files were handed over to the Jewish owners when their properties were returned to them. See Van Doorslaer (ed.), *De bezittingen van de slachtoffers*, pp. 185-186, 212-221.

19 Veerle Vanden Daelen, *Laten we hun lied verder zingen. De heropbouw van de joodse gemeenschap in Antwerpen na de Tweede Wereldoorlog (1944-1960)* (Amsterdam 2008), pp. 53-55.

the circumstances of most victims' deaths, this information was very often impossible to provide. It was not until 1949 that the Dutch parliament enacted a law that regulated death certificates for missing persons who had presumably died in the camps (*Wet houdende voorzieningen betreffende het opmaken van akten van overlijden van vermisten*, J227, 2 June 1949). Only after this law came into force was it possible for people who had lost their spouses during the war to remarry and only then did the widowed spouse of a missing person receive a pension.[20] Only then, too, could inheritances be legalised.

The clause in the Dutch legislation that a person who purchased an asset in good faith had to be compensated for his loss led to difficult situations concerning the recovery of real estate, especially in cities where sales had been more anonymous and where not everybody knew each other when they traded goods. In some cases the property had been sold more than once. In such cases the Immovable Property Division of the Council of Restoration of Rights (*Afdeling Onroerende Goederen van de Raad voor het Rechtsherstel*) had to split the claim between all the buyers, which often proved to be very complex. In principle, Jewish owners recovered their property. However, the owners would never return completely to the *status quo ante*. In cases where the last buyer wanted to retain the property, with the consent of the Jewish original owner, the Jewish claimant received the product of the sale during the war. In cases where the Jewish property had not been sold, but rented by a *Verwalter* to a third party, the returning Jew could find himself in an absurd situation in which he received no income from the property, but nonetheless remained responsible to the tenants for any default.[21]

In Antwerp, however, the vast majority of the Jewish population had rented accommodation.[22] By the time they returned, most of this accommodation had been rented to other people in the meantime. But what about the validity of rental agreements for three, six or nine years that had been abruptly ended in 1942? It was not self-evident that a tenant should vacate his rental accommodation after the liberation for the benefit of the original Jewish tenant who had since returned. The legal decree of January 1941 was valid only in respect of forced terminations of rental agreements at the occupier's command. In practice, however, the situation had been

---

20 Aalders, *Berooid*, pp. 86, 91-92, 366. I would like to thank Professor Laurens Winkel for drawing my attention to this fact during discussions after my lecture at the conference at the Erasmus University of Rotterdam on 28 April 2006.
21 Aalders, *Berooid*, pp. 190-191; W. Veraart, *Ontrechting en rechtsherstel in Nederland en Frankrijk in de jaren van bezetting en wederopbouw* (Deventer 2005), pp. 164-172, 213-216.
22 Van Doorslaer (ed.), *De bezittingen van de slachtoffers*, p. 76; V. Vanden Daelen, 'De houding van de Amerikaanse Joint ten opzichte van de orthodoxie: de Antwerpse casus', *Bijdragen tot de Eigentijdse Herinnering/Cahiers de la Mémoire Contemporaine* 6 (2005), p. 157.

much more subtle during the war, and so the law offered little or no consolation.[23]

A new Rent Act was passed on 12 March 1945. This included a few provisions intended to rectify the situation of Jewish former tenants.[24] Articles 30 to 32 of chapter IV, 'Restoration to some tenants of the possession of the properties previously occupied by them', had particular consequences for the returned Jews. Article 30 referred to the tenant who, under direct or indirect material or moral pressure from the hostile occupying authorities, had felt obliged to leave the property that he had been living in or working from, *without his personal consent*. From now on, a former tenant in this position could ask any present tenant or occupant, even those who were *bona fide*, to give him secured possession of the rented property again.

However, we learn that in 1945-1946 a majority of the justices of the peace ruled against the Jewish claimants because they had supposedly agreed with the termination of the rental agreements. In practice many Jewish tenants had indeed passed their rental agreements on to third parties in order to avoid later being called to account by the owners for non-payment of rent or premature termination of rental agreements. Only a minority of the justices of the peace accepted that these transfers of rental agreements were flawed because of moral pressure. A law of 12 April 1947 introduced a suspicion of absence of *consensus ad idem* to any agreement that was entered into during the occupation by someone being persecuted because of his "race, nationality, political opinion or because of his place of residence."[25] This important amendment of the legal decree of 10 January 1941 made it easier to recover immovable property. Until then, such recuperation had been problematic if the owner had not parted from the property on the explicit and direct order of the occupier. This law changed the aforementioned situation, at least on a legal level. In reality it w as undoubtedly enacted much too late to 'regularise' the old rental agreements. We assume that most Jews who rented their accommodation either found a solution in an amicable arrangement or – most probably – had to look for a new residence. However, this led neither to detailed historical research on the matter, nor to a lively debate within the Jewish community in Belgium.

Research in the Netherlands, elaborated by Veraart, shows that restitution of rented property did not follow a clear and unequivocal path. Judges

---

23 Vanden Daelen, *Laten we hun lied verder zingen*, pp. 56-57.
24 Besluit-wet van 12 maart 1945 waarbij uitzonderingsbepalingen van tijdelijken aard inzake huishuur worden voorzien en waarbij aan de tijdelijke geldigheid van de besluiten van 20 september 1940, 28 april 1941, 18 november 1942 en 15 juli 1943 een einde wordt gemaakt, *Belgisch Staatsblad* (15 March 1945); Erratum, *Belgisch Staatsblad* (23 – 24 April 1945).
25 M. Polain and A. Abrahams, 'Commentaires législatifs. La loi du 12 avril 1947 établissant une présomption légale au profit de certaines personnes victimes de contrainte morale', *Journal des Tribunaux* (1947), pp. 339-344 (See especially art. 3 paragraph 2 *a contrario* for the amendment).

seem to have had a great deal of liberty in which to reach their judgements, and this led to various contradictory results, depending on the specific case and judge. Dutch judges tried to take as many factors as possible into consideration within this social minefield of adjudicating the situation of the Jewish victims, the circumstances in which the present tenants moved into a property and the huge post-war housing shortage.[26]

Recovery of movable property

Shares and other financial assets

The restitution of shares and other financial assets followed a different track in both countries, mostly due to the different way in which each country managed such assets during the war. In Belgium, bank accounts were the only movable property that was relatively easy to recover after the war. Under the act of 31 May 1941, Jews had to identify their financial assets as Jewish.[27] Under the Act of 14 January 1943 all Jewish financial assets had to be centralised at the *Société Française de Banque et de Dépôts* (SFBD) on a blocked bank account in the name of the *Brüsseler Treuhandgesellschaft* (BTG). However, this centralisation operation had not yet been completed by the time of the liberation in September 1944. On 3 March 1943 the *Brüsseler Treuhandgesellschaft* was also put in charge of administering safe deposit boxes: the boxes were registered and emptied in the presence of the owner or a bailiff and a clear report of the contents was made. Of the content of these safe deposit boxes, Belgian currency and shares were also centralised at the SFBD; gold and foreign currencies were transferred to the Emission Bank, while other items were kept at the original bank itself. By the time of the liberation on 4 September 1944, the BTG accounts at the SFBD consisted of 3,365 accounts with balances totalling 138,686,975.03 Belgian Francs and 1,345 securities accounts holding balances of 189,792,749 Belgian Francs. The securities represented almost 58% of the total value.[28] Undeclared financial assets kept at home were probably seized in the *Möbelaktion* and cashed in during the war.

How could Jews in Belgium recover their financial assets after the liberation? If an account had not been identified as Jewish or if a bank had not transferred an account that had been identified as Jewish to the SFBD, the

---

26 Veraart, *Ontrechting en rechtsherstel*, pp. 104-115.
27 The Act of 15 July 1941 stipulated that all Jewish financial assets were to be deposited in a *deviezenbank*, which was a bank licensed by the occupier to trade in foreign currencies and securities and requisitionings as stipulated in the occupant's Act of 17 June 1940. The measure of 15 July 1941 consequently did not have any major consequences. See Van Doorslaer (ed.), *De bezittingen van de slachtoffers*, pp. 42-52.
28 Van Doorslaer (ed.), *De bezittingen van de slachtoffers*, pp. 42-52, 192 and enclosures, p. 35.

assets would still be deposited at the original bank. If an account had indeed been transferred to the SFBD, the account holder simply had to submit a request to the *Dienst van het Sekwester*, after which the assets would be returned. The *Dienst van het Sekwester* never undertook systematic searches for lawful claimants. In order to claim their rights the original owners or their heirs had to initiate such proceedings themselves. Furthermore, the original banks often asked for SFBD accounts to be returned to their bank, not necessarily acting at the request or in the interests of the claimant. By 31 December 1954 the number of centralised bank accounts had fallen to 1,070 (31.7% of the original number), with total balances of 14,286,751.52 Belgian Francs (10% of the original sum), while the number of securities accounts had fallen to 472 (35% of the original accounts), with total balances of 3,119,061 Belgian Francs (1.6% of the original sum). There are two explanations for the substantial decrease in the value of the securities on these centralised accounts. Firstly, the wealthiest Jews, who had had greater chances of surviving, returned and claimed their property. Secondly, securities were the most difficult accounts to administer.[29] In the case of undeclared securities that were cashed in during the war, restitution was almost impossible. In order to avoid trading in securities of suspect origin, the Belgian Ministry of Finance issued an order on 26 May 1945 requiring claimants to prove (in the form, for example, of a stockbroker's declaration) that they had owned the stocks before 10 May 1940.[30] This was definitely not a foolproof measure. There has been a good deal of research concerning the looting of securities in the Netherlands, whereas in Belgium there has been hardly any research into the matter to date.

The reason for this is that the situation in the Netherlands was far more complicated than in Belgium. Unlike Belgium, where Jews only had to identify their bank accounts and shares as Jewish, Jews in the Netherlands had to centralise their financial belongings in Liro, Sarphatistraat, a bank established by the occupier under the same and, therefore, misleading abbreviation as a well known and respected former Jewish bank in the Netherlands, 'Lippman, Rosenthal en Co'. On the orders of the German authorities, Liro actively used these assets and sold shares and other assets on the Amsterdam Stock Exchange from November 1942 onwards. Liro sold to about 100,000 buyers, with the proportion of the value represented by these shares being much higher than in Belgium. According to Liro's own calculations in early August 1944, they accounted for about 75% of the total value deposited at the bank. The restitution process, which immediately received great attention in the Netherlands, was made considerably more complicated by the lack of concrete information on the buyers and the subsequent transactions. There was a lack of legislation on the matter, a fact

---

29 Van Doorslaer (ed.), *De bezittingen van de slachtoffers*, pp. 42-55, 192-199, 396-399.
30 Archief Beurs van Antwerpen, Notulen Beurscommissie, 1 June 1945.

that was aggravated by defects in the laws of inheritance applying in respect of Holocaust victims. The concept of 'good faith' once again led to a great deal of complications. If the stocks were being legally traded, every transaction was also supposed to be legal. However, shares and securities sold by a German spoliation organization could hardly be considered as trade in good faith. Everybody could know what this organization did, and so people could know that these shares and securities must have belonged to Jews.[31] About 90% of the value of these securities was refunded, although only after a long and difficult restitution procedure.[32]

Jewish household effects irrevocably gone

The *Möbelaktion*, or the fact that all Jewish properties were emptied and their contents transported to Germany, was most probably the most painful kind of spoliation. All personal belongings, including all furniture and other household items constituting part of a family's history, were gone, most probably never to be found again. The action was indeed very radical and the German occupier executed this action on a very large scale. Every trace of Jewish presence and existence in Europe was to be erased.[33]

The only consolation that the Belgian legal decree of 10 January 1941 offered was in the case of movable property alienated on the orders of the occupier. The law of 12 April 1947 left more room for manoeuvre: parting with movable property on a 'voluntary' basis through an agreement, such as a sale, under pressure of temporary circumstances could still be undone. Most cases, however, were simply cases of theft, through the *Möbelaktion*. In most cases, Jewish residents' furniture had been collected by the Antwerp removal firm Arthur Pierre, located on Isabellalei in a Jewish neighbourhood. The inventories drawn up during the emptying were generally vague and specified, for example, only the numbers of chairs and tables or the numbers of crates filled with silverware or linen that had been removed.[34]

---

31 Aalders, *Berooid*, pp. 270-274.
32 As previously mentioned, the restitution decree E100 was amended in Decree F272, and this significantly complicated the process. This change in law of 16 November 1945 made every possible buyer of Jewish assets a *bona fide* buyer. It was up to the victim to prove otherwise. In addition, retracing the trail of the assets, through multiple sales on stock exchanges, often proved very difficult, see Aalders, *Berooid*, pp. 158-159, 363: Veraart, *Ontrechting en rechtsherstel*, pp. 219-220, 229).
33 Van Doorslaer (ed.), *De bezittingen van de slachtoffers*, pp. 119.
34 Van Doorslaer (ed.), *De bezittingen van de slachtoffers*, pp. 128-129. Arthur Pierre not only moved furniture, but also, just like a dozen or so other removal firms in Antwerp, transported Jews to Mechelen. Pierre was subsequently tried for collaboration and sentenced to five years' imprisonment. On 5 November 1971 his name was restored to honour by the Brussels Court of Appeal. Not only furniture was collected. Some Antwerp shipping companies kept in their containers the possessions of Jews who had left

After the war the *Dienst Economische Recuperatie* (Economic Recuperation Service) was established in order to trace and restitute goods and to organise compensation for the victims if such measures were legally founded.[35] For the Jewish victims this service brought little consolation: very little Jewish property was restituted or compensated.[36] Victims were clearly advised that they had to file a report with the police in order to qualify for possible compensation. Innumerable reports can be found in the Antwerp police records in which returned Jews drew up inventories of their property and indicated who was the likely suspect to have emptied their homes and the approximate time that this would have happened.

In the end very few movable possessions were ever recovered, which raises the question of compensation. The law of 1 October 1947 on war damage to private property was valid only for people with Belgian nationality. However, most Jews in Belgium – more than 90% – were technically not Belgian citizens. The World Jewish Congress (WJC) tried to persuade the Belgian government to amend this legislation in 1951, and substantiated its argumentation with examples and laws from other European countries,[37] but these attempts failed. Most Jews in Belgium had to wait for the *BrüG*-law (*Bundesrückerstattungsgesetz*) of 19 July 1957, a German federal law on restitution and compensation.

In the Netherlands, as well, very little removable property was ever recovered. The Liro bank had a card system of jewellery and personal assets, but this list was not detailed enough for an asset ever to be recovered through it. Given the low chances of recovering any household furniture, the Dutch government did not even establish a special recuperation commission. It was practically impossible to recognise tables, chairs and couches, let alone silverware and plates. Even the destination of removed property was generally impossible to trace. In a few cases victims were offered compensation. The whole problem with such damage claims was that the claimants did not have documents to prove the goods they had once owned.[38]

---

the country before the occupation and who wanted their household effects shipped abroad afterwards. During the war these goods were also confiscated. After the liberation there was virtually no chance of retracing these household effects.

35 AJA, WJC-files, C247/3, Belgium, indemnification and reparations, 1945, La récupération des biens meubles en Belgique et en Allemagne, S. Wolkowicz to Comité des Juifs de Belgique, 13 September 1945.
36 Van Doorslaer (ed.), *De bezittingen van de slachtoffers*, pp. 237-255.
37 AJA, WJC-files, H59/19, Belgium, correspondence, topics, heirless property, 1950-1951.
38 Aalders, *Berooid*, pp. 171, 176, 203-207.

Assets placed in safekeeping

During the war many Jews hid securities, money, jewels and diamonds in cellars, behind wallpaper or in hidden compartments. Because of the *Möbelaktion* they also tried to leave furniture with non-Jewish neighbours and friends. After their return they tried to recover these possessions as quickly as possible in order to have some means of existence. Often, however, it was impossible to recover these assets immediately.

In many cases someone else had hidden the securities, which made it difficult to determine precisely where they were hidden. Moreover, other people had often moved into these properties, which meant that returning Jews depended on the goodwill of the new residents to provide them with access to their former residences. Those who had doubts about this goodwill went first to the police to make a declaration and to request a search of their homes in order to find the securities. Others went straight to the houses where their property was believed to be hidden. Some residents let the Jews tell their story first and then refused to let them search their houses.[39]

During the war some property was given into the care of people, usually non-Jews, deemed trustworthy. Specialised Dutch literature uses the term *bewariërs* (a contraction of '*bewaren*', Dutch for keeping/preserving, and '*Ariër*', Dutch for Aryan, meaning 'Aryan guardians'), a term we will also use here. There were certainly good *bewariërs* who returned everything upon the return of the owners or their rightful heirs. Unfortunately, there were also cases where the *bewariër* agreement posed problems, not least when the original owner had not returned after the war. Some *bewariërs* wished to restitute the goods only to the person who had originally given them and not to anyone who professed to act on behalf of that person.[40] In such cases there was no option but to wait for the legal declaration of the owner's death. Other instances were even more disillusioning. Some *bewariërs*, having anticipated that the original owners would not return, had sold the goods or were otherwise unwilling to return possessions that had been left in their care. Michal Citroen, among others, recorded testimonies about these facts in the Netherlands.[41]

In Belgium, requesting the return of assets was likewise often difficult and often led to disappointments and problems. Some *bewariërs* even denied ever having received the goods that had been entrusted to them. Often the goods had already been passed on or sold, and investigations were

---

39 For example: Stadsarchief Antwerpen, Politiearchief, Processen-verbaal 7de wijk, MA 29 933/2001.
40 'Les enfants abandonnés et les biens sans maître', *Ofipresse* 28 (14 December 1945), p. 2.
41 'Stichting Onderzoek Terugkeer en Opvang' already mentioned this problem explicitly in its 'Onderzoeksplan' of May 1999. See also Citroen, *U wordt door niemand verwacht*, pp. 158-159; Aalders, *Berooid*, pp. 337-340.

required to retrace them. Sometimes the *bewariërs* no longer lived at the same address. In those cases the only option for Jewish owners was to file a case with the police. There are cases where requests to return certain possessions provoked violence. Sometimes claimants were simply thrown out onto the street, as the Antwerp police records show:

> "We went downstairs again [when the furniture that had been placed in safekeeping was not found] and I opened the front door. The father [S.] slammed it shut again in my husband's face and pulled his beard and pushed him against the wall. [S.] yelled at us that he would see to it anyway that both my husband and I would be put in a concentration camp, to which my husband replied that in that case he would have to wait until the Germans came back."[42]

Typical for such cases was that the other party usually disputed the facts. Cases like these probably caused Jews to warn each other that it was not as easy as they had thought to recover property they had entrusted to others and that it was wise in such cases to involve the police (although some Jews were too quick to involve the police).[43] It was often a case of one person's word against another's, and it was difficult if not impossible to prove ownership. As a consequence some Jews did not even bother to try to recover their possessions. We do not know how many *bewariërs* betrayed the Jewish confidence, but this is certainly part of the trauma that has already been put into words very clearly in numerous studies in the Netherlands, but which in Belgium has remained private. The only way to retrace these facts in Belgium is by searching police records.

Concluding remarks and explanatory hypothesis

The consequences of the war were harsh, and the impact of the isolation and persecution of the Jewish population was severe. All too often this part of history is forgotten, which means that for many Jews the war did not really end at the liberation. It took a very long time, too long, for this restitution to be carried out, but in the end Dutch researchers such as Gerard Aalders have classified the restitution in the Netherlands as "positive in moderate terms" (in other words, compensation of almost 90%, but only after a long wait).[44] The relatively long time (longer than in Belgium) that elapsed before the Dutch government arranged for declarations of presumable death of deported Jews surely played a significant part in delaying the Dutch restitution process, as did the amendment of the law for resti-

---

42 Stadsarchief Antwerpen, Politiearchief, Processen-verbaal 7de wijk, MA 29 936/2705. (Translated from Dutch)
43 For example: Stadsarchief Antwerpen, Politiearchief, Processen-verbaal 7de wijk, MA 29 923/3136.
44 Aalders, *Berooid*, p. 368.

tuting securities. According to Aalders, the reproaches of bureaucracy, legalism, formalism and the 'cold' approach – where the last two are consequences of the first two – cannot be seen as a failure of the restitution. These contributed a great deal to the negative image of the restitution process, while the long waiting times and bureaucratic treatment were undoubtedly very distressing for the victims, but all this does not affect the final result of restoring 90% of the belongings.[45]

In Belgium, attention – both academically and from within the Jewish population – for the material consequences of the war for Jews has arisen only in recent years, whereas in the Netherlands the subject has been studied and discussed extensively. This can be explained by two closely related facts: nationality and the degree of assimilation. Jews in the Netherlands were generally Dutch citizens and were largely assimilated, whereas Jews in Belgium often held only temporary residence permits and were usually less assimilated, especially those who were orthodox. Not only did these factors result in a different attitude of the respective governments, but Jews also had considerably different expectations of their respective governments. Jews in Belgium formed a minority of the population and only a minority of this minority had Belgian nationality, which meant their influence on political decision making was very limited. Jews in Belgium also tried to organize themselves as independently as possible in order not to attract the State's attention. They were afraid that becoming a burden on the Belgian state would reduce their chances of becoming citizens. Any form of help was welcome, but not expected.[46] Dutch Jews, on the other hand, had high expectations of receiving State support in order to rectify the injustices done to them. As Dutch citizens, they had put their trust in their government and fellow citizens to offer support. The trauma caused by their not having received a warm welcome – often they received the exact opposite – and by the bureaucratic treatment of their files and assets was huge. Their disappointment in the Dutch government led to complaints, testimonies, books and academic research.[47] However, even though Jews in the Netherlands generally had Dutch nationality, they were not a significant electoral group. They remained a minority that, in political terms, was almost negligible and hence did not receive much political attention.[48] The spoliation during the war and the difficult restitution afterwards were similar in both countries, but led to – at least – two different reactions in Belgium and the Nether-

---

45 Aalders, *Berooid*, pp. 331-335, 355, 366.
46 Vanden Daelen, *Laten we hun lied verder zingen*, pp. 60, 264-266.
47 Aalders, *Berooid*, p. 331; Veraart, *Ontrechting en rechtsherstel*, p. 73.
48 Aalders, *Berooid*, p. 356. The fact that most Jews in the Netherlands were Dutch nationals also comes to the fore in this study. 'Foreign Jews' are a small part (three short paragraphs) of the whole study. Apparently these foreign Jews in the Netherlands were mostly German-Jewish refugees and were as a group apparently too small to merit more time and space within the study. See Aalders, *Berooid*, pp. 340-341).

lands, primarily due to the degree of integration, assimilation and national citizenship of Jews in the respective countries.

The Goudstikker Case

Herman C.F. Schoordijk[*]

The case of Goudstikker that ended in 2006[1] must have led jurists to the insight that the use of legal dogmatics cannot be missed in solving practical legal problems. In this respect the jurist can be compared with a surgeon who works without emotions. The jurist has to apply the law and has to resist the temptation of using unessential arguments of legal politics too early. In this way we must look at the restitution cases of the post-war period. Until recently this was not possible because we did not possess all the information as for example in the Goudstikker case. A full report of the case is now available due to the efforts of the Advisory Committee on the Assessment of Restitution Applications for items of Cultural Value and the Second World War (Restitution Committee).[2] Although the report is quite detailed, there are more documents in the Netherlands Institute for War Documentation (NIOD) which could shed greater light on the question and possibly leading to slightly different interpretations. This, however, is not very likely. The report, as such, is straightforward and does not contain legal conclusions but it shows that all individuals involved have committed elementary juridical mistakes. Simply put: the law has not been applied in a correct way. The trustee of the Miedl-patrimony, the later member of the Supreme Court E.J. Korthals Altes and the attorney for the State, the famous attorney D.J. Veegens who represented the Dutch State via the National Trust Fund (*Nederlands Beheersinstituut, NBI*), showed an appalling lack of elementary legal knowledge. I am still frightened by this shocking fact and I will come back to this in § 1. But there is no doubt about the ethical standards and the consideration of those involved: Veegens[3], Korthals Altes and others did their outmost and were concerned with the fate of the persecuted Jews. They apparently complied with the wishes of the Minister of Finance, Lieftinck, who placed the economic recovery of the Netherlands above the justified interests of the Jews and many other war victims. Were they struck with blindness or is the situation different for the

---

[*] A Dutch version of this article has been published in *Nederlands Juristenblad* (2006), pp. 743-748. Translation by Laurens Winkel.
[1] See www.restitutiecommissie.nl.
[2] See the Advisory Committee on the Assessment of Restitution Applications for Items of Cultural Value and the Second World War, *Goudstikker-Report* (RC 1.15) (in Dutch), (The Hague 2006) and the Advisory Committee on the Assessment of Restitution Applications for Items of Cultural Value and the Second World War, *Goudstikker-Recommendation* (RC 1.15) (in Dutch) (The Hague 2006).
[3] See the interview with him in Jan M. van Dunné, *Acht civilisten in burger* (Zwolle 1977), pp. 237–275.

representative of the Goudstikker family, the attorney Max Meijer? Did he follow a good strategy or was he struck with the same blindness? Is the tragic patrimonial fate of the Goudstikker heirs a consequence of 'the frivolous rule' already mentioned in the lecture rooms and – so to speak – 'reconfirmed' in a court decision of the Court of Appeal of The Hague to which we will return later: The judge pronounces his verdict, impartially; but he does take into account the person of the attorney?

1. What was the subject matter?

As probably the most influential Amsterdam art dealer, Goudstikker was – just as many of the other Jewish bankers and traders and many others who had reasons to fear a German invasion and occupation – rather well aware of German plans. He planned to escape and designated beforehand Dr Sternheim LL.M as his representative. The latter died 10 May 1940 at the very moment Goudstikker, together with his wife and child boarded the boat for England. Goudstikker himself died during the voyage due to an accident on May 16. *Inde lacrimae.*

An employee with supervision of the art gallery at Castle Nijenrode for many years, A.A. ten Broek, took over as a trustee of the whole art collection. He started collaborating with the German banker and businessman Alois Miedl who had already settled in the Netherlands long before the war and was a good friend of Hermann Göring. The latter drew his attention immediately after the capitulation – as it turned out in many other documents which I studied – to the art collections, because he wanted to acquire them and wanted to sell of some parts.

This led to two transactions: the selling of the shares of the art collection enterprise and the selling of a great part of the collection itself to Göring. To start with the latter; A.A. ten Broek sold the collection on paper to Göring on July 1, but in reality Miedl had sold the collection earlier with the help of Ten Broek. In this case, bribery played a role, a circumstance as mentioned in art. 1371 of the Dutch Civil Code. This could arguably be proved by the fact that Miedl - and not Göring - gave him a commission fee of DFL 180.000, an amount thirty times the usual salary for high officials and ministers in the Netherlands. This fact was thoroughly mistrusted by the later trustee of Miedl's patrimony Korthals Altes, but he did not take this into account during his fulfilment of the trust of Miedl's patrimony.

The shares of the art collecting enterprise were also sold to Miedl by Ten Broek with the consent of the general assembly of shareholders of NV Goudstikker. But who were voting there at that moment? The mother of Goudstikker who owned 50 shares, voted in favour and acquired with this consent the protection of Miedl and Göring for her personal and patrimonial safety. The other voter in favour of the transfer was A.A. ten Broek who was entitled to vote because the NV Goudstikker bought 250 of its own shares. The widow of Goudstikker sent a telegram saying she was opposed to the sale to Miedl. There were no other shares with the right to vote at that moment.

The heirs of Goudstikker had on paper a very strong case after the war. Both sales of the company and the collection to Göring were void on grounds already indicated and for those who still hesitate: the London Decree A6 of 1940 forbade all transactions with the enemy and declared them null and void. The ownership of the company and the collection could not be legally transferred to German hands and remained Goudstikker's property. The state was to be left with empty hands. The result on the basis of art. 1371 Civil Code and the Decree A6 should have been the following: the company and the collection fell back to the heirs of Goudstikker who at the same time had a claim based on tort against Miedl. All payments to the company should be returned. None of the *dramatis personae* seemed to be aware of the Decree A6, except for one moment. The attorney Max Meijer who during three years negotiated on behalf of the heirs with the powerful trust NBI who could be considered *ex officio* as the *beatus possidens*, seemed to wake up only September 21, 1948. Tired of further negotiations he wrote on February 3, 1947[4] that he was about to leave talking about a settlement and to invoke the decision of the normally competent judge in view of testing the compatibility of the sales with the articles of Decree A6, but in doing so, he forgot that the normal judge was not competent in this kind of case (according to art. 16 Decree E100, 1944). A special court had been instituted for this type of claim: the Judicial Division of the Council for the Restoration of Rights (*Raad voor het Rechtsherstel, Afdeling Rechtspraak*). This remained only a thread and it did not prevent the heirs to conclude a peaceful settlement approved by NBI. In return the widow paid DFL 379.855 to Miedl whose patrimony was under the administration of NBI in order to obtain restitution of the immovable property (Herengracht and castle Nijenrode). It is the cart pulling the horse.[5]

Meijers' proposals concerning the restitution of the shares of the art trade company are doubtful as well. The heirs started the negotiations February 4, 1947, and made the comment that a full restitution would not be possible

> "[...] because there is no business company anymore that could be restituted and secondly because a part of the patrimony that has been transferred by Miedl is no longer there."

---

4 *Goudstikker-Report*, nr. 3.2.4.
5 *Goudstikker-Report*, p. 18

This is certainly not correct. Restitution of all transactions always remained possible for the reasons of nullity based on A6 and section 1371 of the Dutch Civil Code according to the general principles of private law.

Until this point I have left out the remarkable fate of the Decree A6. Subsequent governments based themselves on art. 10, second clause of A6[6] – written for a very different purpose – and did not hesitate to leave aside A6 by deciding that property sold to Germans that was under the spell of A6 still Dutch property, was declared German enemy property which could be taken by the Dutch state. This is hardly to be believed. Certainly, this decision was in favour of the Dutch economy, but at the same time it is clearly contrary to the provision in the Constitution holding that expropriation is only possible by statute and under very specific guarantees. In short: unlawful. It is also evident that an appeal to the European Court of Human Rights, Strasbourg, could very well be successful.

2. Counter Indications for restitution?

On August 1 1952 an out-of-court settlement[7] was concluded between Goudstikker's widow Desi and the NBI stating that she waived every restitutionary claim regarding the sale of the art trading company and the sale of a number of paintings to Miedl. The largest part of the art collection sold to Göring (the so-called collection-Göring) was finally not included in the settlement, which scope was limited to the transactions with Miedl. Remarkable fact was that the NBI hesitated to approve the settlement until the moment there also was a settlement with Miedl concerning his enemy-status. The final version only came about after the discussion of several drafts the first of which included the Göring-collection but this so-called Göring-transaction was eventually left out of the settlement.

The NBI and the trustee of Miedl abstained from ownership of more than 300 pieces of art in exchange of a payment of Dfl. 102.000 in the presence of the notary public E. Spier. The deed starts with a *considerans* which we rarely find in notary deeds. Is there a reason for this? *Lex est quodcumque notamus*. A *considerans* can only lead to interpretation of the deed. Such is the prevailing opinion and the opinion of still too many, nowadays. The notary public does not want interpretation of the notary deeds. How different is our opinion now and how different are our thoughts on the – in the past often abused – notarial professional secret. In short, the long *considerans* contains the following. Desi Goudstikker declared that she was very tired. She says so not literally but this is the quintessence of her declaration. She is dreading the further quarrelling for years 'also conside-

---

6   The text in translation: 'The nullity as meant in the previous clause can be lifted by the Commission through a validation of a contract or a legal act.'
7   *Goudstikker-Report*, p. 29.

ring the actual insecure political situation'. She declared further that she could not share any of the arguments until now used by the NBI and she felt very much prejudiced. Before the restitution in 2006 the general opinion was that the heirs of Goudstikker were without a chance because of the settlement. I think that this *considerans* proves 'undue influence'; a potential reason to declare the settlement null and void - and after 1992 "prone to annulment". There is indeed undue influence, especially because the state has taken possession of the art collection by unlawful use of the Decree A6. The Restitution Committee holds a different view. The settlement was concluded with free will. This is begging the question. The Committee, using political terms, hints that there was no undue influence and gives as reasoning the following: Goudstikker chose of two civil possibilities the less harmful one. This, however, is not a correct way of reasoning. The old contracts in the Commercial Code prove this very well. In a case of shipwrecking, a captain concludes contracts with intervening ships. The captain chooses the lesser evil of the two: going to wreck or concluding a contract, but this contract is the school example of rescission (section 555 Dutch Commercial Code-Old) and of undue influence. The Restitution Committee uses practically no legal language, but this does not conceal the lack of conviction. The heirs of Goudstikker have been prejudiced by this unfair argumentation. The Miedl-settlement remains intact. I cannot see whether there are other political arguments. Sometimes a solution is just, but, according to Gustav Radbruch and the Dutch lawyer M.H. Bregstein, we need to understand a lawyer, a judge and in this case the Restitution Committee better than they do it themselves and we even have to look for better arguments. The further arguments used to renounce the revision of the Miedl settlement are not convincing either. The Committee explains what the characteristics of the settlement are and puts emphasis on the fact that it ended a legal procedure in the Council of Restitution. There had been unconditional renunciation of property rights. But all those arguments do not make sense when the preliminary question (under which falls the undue influence) has been solved incorrectly.

The Göring collection was completely restored to the heirs. Praiseworthy, are the arguments and the empathy shown by the committee. However, I have heard less praiseworthy reactions. After the completion in the Goudstikker case there were rumours about Jewish pressure. American museums especially such as Getty do not want to deal with policies and politics; they want to hear whether the law has been applied correctly. Minister Donner had a problem when the Committee gave its advice. Maybe a judicial decision has been cancelled. The rule of law is endangered. The state would have to face an avalanche of legal restitutionary claims. In the weekend of 5-6 February 2006 he put attorneys and legal specialists to work to sort this out and especially to save the last verdict of the Hague Court of Appeal. This court had ruled that restitution of neither of the two collections was possible. It used mainly two arguments: we are not competent as Court of Appeal because the Secretary of State is not a part of the post war Restitution Court. Secondly, the claims have expired due to the law of prescription. *Motu proprio* the claim of restitution was not honoured either. Finally the verdict of the Court of Appeal was put aside as to the Göring collection with the reasoning that the Court could not have sentenced according to the newly developed standards for restitution.

During the press conference the Government stressed that the decision for restitution was based on morals, not on law. In the meantime it is becoming less clear what the limits of the new policy of restitution are.

3. Question marks to the restitution policy guidelines.

Lites finiri oportet. Why should we be mild with former judicial decisions as is apparently advocated by Minister Donner? In Land-Eggens we read a passage by Eggens directed against those who speak of incorrect judicial decisions. According to him we are not allowed to do so: what the judge says is the law. But this does not exclude that positive morality may require that a party behaves as if there was a misjudgement. The state has a special position here. It can make suggestions and acts as a role model. The state has more patrimonial sustainability than the individual. Criminal cases can be reviewed as well, especially when there is "nova". Therefore, it is the duty of the Ministry of Justice and the Restitution Committee not only to overrule judgments based on new legal insights, but also to reopen old cases when there is new evidence as appears from time to time in the accounts of the restitution committees. In the mean time one could ask whether the now established guidelines are clear and practical and above all, enhance justice. They are derived from the recommendations of the Committee Ekkart and fully accepted by the government. Recommendation 1 entails, in short, that judgments made cannot be reversed unless there are *nova*. Recommendation 2 clarifies how to interpret this. The Committee

> "…advises to enlarge the notion of *nova* as it was understood until now in practice and to define it also as deviations in view of earlier judgments of the Restitution Council, and to extend it to the results of changed historical insights as to the legal correctness and consequences of the policy of the post war era."

If the recommendations of the committee should be read in the sense that earlier judgments should remain intact and the guidelines should only be applied in future to undecided cases (the apparent opinion of the Minister of Justice Donner) one can only say that the creation of the Committee does not respond to the many international appeals to give justice to those who lost their property in the Second World War. This narrow view will not be understood. The NBI did not act as a service institute for those who lost their property in wartime, but – seen the perverted interpretation of the Royal Decree A 6 – as an institute that favoured the interests of the State too much. The creation of the Restitution Committee must not be seen as mere lip service to new insights on post war justice. This cannot be its proper interpretation.

How could historical insight as to the justice of the restitution policy until this day be defined? In the new policy the echo of the enormous changes in private law theory after 1970 had to be heard. These changes of legal culture were the object of my research which culminated in my report to the Royal Academy of Sciences in 2005.[8] Before the Second World War there was a lot of progress in jurisprudence which was not reflected in legal practice for a long time. Even a brilliant legal scholar as M.H. Bregstein had too narrow a view on the role of equity after the war, when he speaks in his well known address as Rector Magnificus at the University of Amsterdam about the moderate role of the statute.[9] For some time now I have found myself unable to agree with this anymore. The statute must not have a moderate role or relative value, but is in principle 100 % binding. The wording of the statute, however, has to be interpreted so that it has convincing force. Insights into the theory of language and interpretation fully allow this view (Gadamer/Wittgenstein). The rigid distinction between voluntary and involuntary does not fit this manner of interpretation. Here we must find the cause of all troubles in cases of post-war restitution.

Perhaps the most important insight of the post-war time is that a new legal doctrine has evolved in which critical distance is created towards the earlier focus on intention. The old and not always well understood concentration on intention was predominant in the 19th century and was previously unknown. This has largely been ignored by the Restitution Council. It is even worse: the State was able to play the role of unapproachable *beatus possessor* through manipulation of the Royal Decree A 6, a fact until now insufficiently disclosed. The Council has therefore concluded in many cases too hastily that there was intentional transfer from a position of free will.

It is necessary to see the facts in their context when answering the question whether restitution is necessary. This should be self evident in our time, but fine tuning in appreciating the facts still is a rare phenomenon. After the presidency of the Supreme Court of Dubbink who was an admirer of Professor I.H. Hijmans[10], in 1981 we see a Copernican change in the decisions

---

8   H.C.F. Schoordijk, 'De privaatrechtelijke rechtscultuur van de twintigste eeuw in context' ('The culture of private law in the 20th century in context'), *Mededeling KNAW* (Amsterdam 2005).
9   M.H. Bregstein, 'De betrekkelijke waarde der wet', in: *Verzameld werk van M.H. Bregstein* (Zwolle 1960), pp. 1–34.
10 Professor of Roman Law at the University of Amsterdam before World War II and an expert in private international law. He developed an original legal theory based on a

of the civil chamber of the Supreme Court: facts are placed far better in their context. This contextualization is very essential in the re-evaluation of post-war restitution cases. That is why research in the archives is often necessary. But are there enough possibilities for this and are there not legal barriers here based on privacy legislation? If the Minister of Justice claims that in old cases revision is not possible, the Second Chamber (Upper House) of Parliament should give its opinion. It can be predicted that a too narrow approach will not be understood anymore, which on the other hand does not imply that sixty years of restitution must be redone completely. It should be possible to mark boundaries without giving in on the level of justice. In some cases therefore restitution will have to be denied, but the old *ars boni et aequi* must be leading here to find appropriate and measured solutions.

4. *Facit*

It is not appropriate to say that the decisions of the Restitution Committee fit in a society based on "sorry arguments". "Sorry" without restitution is essentially different from "sorry" with restitution. A new policy is very necessary, for the post war restitution was too dominated by the powerful position of the State and was therefore often unjust.

The statutory rules of restitution laid down in the Royal Decrees E 100 and E 133 are not in themselves the cause of the deficit in restitutionary cases. Suyling and I have praised Eggens extensively for his London based legislation on restitution, to which pre-war innovations in legal dogmatics very much contributed. These innovations played again a predominant and fruitful role in the creation of the New Civil Code in 1992. Even nowadays one can learn from them. Veraart is contesting this in his well written doctoral dissertation devoted to restitution cases after the war[11] with the argument that according to Dutch restitution statutes and contrary to the normal rule, third parties are protected in cases of involuntary loss of possession. This was different in the restitution laws of France. The Dutch legislator in London adopted many views which later were incorporated in the Civil Code of 1992. Eggens could not foresee the political background of the post-war restitution practice in which the financial interests of the state in view of the economic revival of the Netherlands would be so predominant.

But we could say that Eggens in London did not evaluate correctly how the legal profession would operate with his open norms in a legal climate – as I stated earlier – dominated by legal positivism. Until then the literal

---

close examination of the facts ('Recht der werkelijkheid'). See T.J. Veen, 'Introductie', in: T.J. Veen & P.C. Kop, *Zestig Juristen, Bijdragen tot een beeld van de geschiedenis der Nederlandse rechtswetenschap* (Zwolle 1987), p. 78.

11 W.J. Veraart, *Ontrechting en rechtsherstel in Nederland en Frankrijk in de jaren van bezetting en wederopbouw* (Deventer 2005).

meaning of the statutory provision was the first source of the judicial decision and legal thinking based on good faith which created judge-made law with convincing force, only had limited significance. The early decision *Baris vs Riezenkamp*[12] in which new perspectives on pre-contractual behaviour were opened was not immediately leading for other cases. The decision was not well received for quite a long time. Our views on how to behave legally have changed and are still changing. The recent court decision of the Supreme Court[13] illustrates this. The reply "Tu l'as voulu" or ""You wanted this so badly" has become far less important.

Professor Oppenheim and W.G. Belinfante, both in London during the war and busy with the drafts of the restitutionary legislation, did not like the frequent invocation of equity. Often the lack of legal certainty was used as an excessively abstract argument against it. Veraart mentions this as well. But, as Eggens used to say, lack of certainty about the law implies – at least on the level of argumentation – certainty about injustice. Eggens used this one-liner following his master Molengraaff. However, Oppenheim and Belinfante both belonged to another school that was loosing support in the Netherlands, which happened here much later than in the common law countries and in Germany. Equity is in bad hands when used by those who do not recognize and fully understand the derogative role of good faith and the famous decision of the Dutch Supreme Court in the Haviltex-case[14] (1981). They are, in fact, obscuring the actual legal discourse.

In short we can conclude: Rules of private law have never been correctly applied by the National Trust Fund NBI: it is not more complicated than this.

---

12 *Nederlandse Jurisprudentie* 1958, 67.
13 Hoge Raad (Supreme Court of the Netherlands) 25 November 2005, *Rechtspraak van de Week* 2005, 132.
14 Hoge Raad (Supreme Court of the Netherlands) in Ermes vs Haviltex, *Nederlandse Jurisprudentie* 1981, 635.

Risks of Open Norms. A Reply to Schoordijk

Arend SOETEMAN

I will not discuss Goudstikker or the history of the restitution of property rights of the Jews. I read the book of Veraart, but apart from that I never did a study on this particular topic. Rather I want to speak about a more general point. In his contribution on Goudstikker in the present volume, Schoordijk evaluates the legal decrees concerning the Dutch restitution of property rights, prepared during the war in London by Eggens, positively. He praised it to the skies, he even writes. Even now we can learn a lot of it. Eggens, Schoordijk says, could not anticipate that the post-war policy on restitution was dominated by a government which considered economic recovery as its top priority. The criticism on open norms about their harming legal certainty is answered by the one-liner that this so-called legal certainty is certainty about injustice.[1]

This one-liner is not confirmed by Veraart's research.[2] To my mind one of the merits of Veraart's book (apart from all the important points on the history of restitution of property rights) is that it illustrates how dangerous open norms can be. In this specific case the legal uncertainty of open norms became the instrument of certain injustice. If the Dutch government and other powerful players in the field (insurance companies, banks, the stock exchange) are not sensitive to the specific and systematic injustice done to the Jews by their being placed outside the legal system (explained by Veraart in his first chapter[3]), if, moreover, economic recovery has political priority, then the open norms clear the way for decisions which do not take the rights of the deprived Jews seriously.

I am inclined to believe that most, if not all, of the judges in the Judicial Division of the Dutch Council of Restoration of Rights were in good faith. If they were inclined to protect third owners of looted goods they probably believed that it was just to protect them, more just than to restore the former Jewish owners in their property rights. Most of us now believe this to be an error in justice. We have to concede that it is always easier to see what justice requires when we look from a distance. Nevertheless, they should have seen, but they did not. How was this possible? How did it come about that trained judges were so blind for what seems obvious to us? Having read Veraart my conjecture is that the Decree on the Restoration of Legal

---

1 See Schoordijk, *supra*, p. 117.
2 Wouter Veraart, *Ontrechting en rechtsherstel in Nederland en Frankrijk in de jaren van bezetting en wederopbouw* (Deventer 2005). For a summary of this research, see also his contribution elsewhere in this book (*supra*, p. 21-34).
3 Veraart, *Ontrechting en rechtsherstel*.

Relations[4], by giving reasonability and equity so central a place, was part of the cause. All over the world the substance of reasonability and equity as a matter of fact quite often is determined by general public opinion, which in its turn quite often is determined by dominant groups. The fact that the dominant groups in this particular case had their own interests in the matter is another part of the cause.

I have general misgivings about open norms, referring to equity or good faith. Unfortunately this specific case of the restitution of property to the Jewish owners confirms my misgivings. The one-liner that connects the relative legal certainty of less abstract norms with certainty of injustice presupposes that we all know and agree about justice and injustice. But that is not the case. Justice is an essentially contestable concept. Moreover, judges have no privileged knowledge about justice. Referring the judge to reasonability and equity is referring the judge to essentially contested concepts. It asks the judge to apply his sense of justice, which very well might differ from the sense of justice of other judges or of some of the parties concerned.

I wish to add that I do not believe that judicial interpretation is, or should be, mainly grammatical. I agree with Schoordijk that we can say with Wittgenstein and Gadamer, but (I add) also with lawyers as Scholten and Dworkin, that the meaning of a text can be much more than, and sometimes even completely different from, what the author could think about. Legal interpretation quite often is and always should be teleological, taking into account the principles behind the law. The judge who interprets the law according to the principles which are made concrete in the law is, I believe, more faithful to the law than the judge who follows the letter or some original intent. We could say that he is applying the reasonability and equity as laid down in the law. But having said this, I also have to say that a judge need some material to interpret teleologically. If the guidance by the law is insufficient, there are problems. For example, Art. 22 of the Decree on the Restoration of Legal Relations invokes the concept that the judge may dispense with a legal provision if the strict application of that provision would lead to conflict with general standards of reasonableness and equity.[5] Consequently, while the law is prepared to subordinate its provisions to reasonableness and equity, it fails to provide the judge concrete formulae of these standards to apply (apart from the judge's own view or the view of some important groups, as to what is reasonable and equitable).

Perhaps I am too strict. Perhaps Eggens did not intend to say that the law might be corrected by reasonability and equity. We should distinguish between two interpretations of these much praised twins. First, the law itself

---

4   The Dutch Decree on the Restoration of Legal Relations ('*Besluit Herstel Rechtsverkeer*', Staatsblad E100) was promulgated on September 17, 1944. For more details, see Veraart, *Ontrechting en rechtsherstel*, pp. 63-67.
5   Veraart, *Ontrechting en rechtsherstel*, p. 582.

determines what is reasonable and equitable according to the law. We may use the letters of the law to discover this reasonability and equity which is explicitly or implicitly formulated in the law. I am a strong supporter of this first reasonability and equity. Second, reasonability and equity can be used as an independent standard to improve or correct the law. This reasonability and equity is sometimes taken from the case itself (*ius in causa positum*), from the circumstances, from our (but whose?) sense of justice, and so on. In the interpretation of the Restitution on Legal Rights Decree, as I understand from Veraart's book, the second interpretation was dominant. My criticism concerns this reasonability and equity which is used to correct or improve the law.

It is a mistake to suppose that open norms referring to a reasonability and equity which could be discovered somehow independent of the law promote justice. They promote that like cases are judged differently by judges with different views, which is unjust. They promote that legal decisions are very sensitive to public opinion or opinion of dominant groups, which under circumstances might be unjust as well. They promote that legal decisions are as capricious as fashions in trends of thought, which is unjust. They promote that our insensitivity to the injustice done to other persons influences our judicial decisions, which is unjust.

If we follow Veraart's book, then all this is exactly what happened with the restitution of property rights in the Netherlands after the Second World War. Dominant groups were far too successful in convincing the judge about their interpretation of reasonability and equity. That was made possible because the law was not clear enough in determining the rights of the original owners who were systematically deprived of their rights.

My valuation of the Dutch Decree on the Restoration of Legal Relations therefore is much more negative than Schoordijk's valuation. Behind this difference of opinion might be a deep difference about the relation between law and judge. I still agree with Montesquieu that it is important for the freedom of the citizens that we separate legislative and judicial power, and that the legislator should make the law which the judge should apply. I do not share naïve views according to which interpretation should follow the grammar of the text or the intentions of the original legislators. The judge should use all his brains and his sensitivity in the application. Sometimes the judge has to follow new paths, which the legislator has not paved already. But if he replaces the legislator's decision about justice by his own view, or if the legislator informs the judge that he has to decide according to reasonability and equity (that is: his own considered view on reasonability and equity), then we are on dangerous paths.

Authors

Claire Andrieu is professor at the Centre for History at the Paris Institute of Political Studies and a former member of the Mattéoli Commission ('Mission Mattéoli'), researching spoliation and restitution of Jewish assets in France during and after the Holocaust period.

Georg Graf is professor of Private Law at the Paris-Lodron University of Salzburg, chairman of Vienna's Wiesenthal Institute for Holocaust Studies (VWI), and a former member of the Historical Commission of the Republic of Austria, investigating the restitution of assets to Nazi victims in post-war Austria.

Jürgen Lillteicher is manager of the Willy Brandt House in Lübeck and fellow at the United States Holocaust Memorial Museum. He conducted the research project 'The Restitution of Jewish Property in Postwar Germany (1945-1969)' at the Charles H. Revson Foundation, has been researcher at the Bucerius Center in Haifa, Israel, and a fellow at the Simon Dubnow Institute for Jewish History and Culture at the Leipzig University. In 2007, his PhD-thesis 'Robbery, Law and Restitution. The Restitution of Jewish Property in the early Federal Republic' (in German) has been published by Wallstein Verlag, Göttingen.

Franz-Stefan Meissel is professor of Roman Law and History of European Private Law at the University of Vienna and former Director of Research for the Historical Commission of the Republic of Austria, investigating the restitution of assets to Nazi victims in post-war Austria.

Herman C.F. Schoordijk is emeritus professor of Private Law at Tilburg University and emeritus professor of Anglo-American Law at the University of Amsterdam. He is a member of the Royal Netherlands Academy of Sciences.

Arend Soeteman is professor of law at the VU University Amsterdam and a member of the Royal Netherlands Academy of Sciences.

Veerle Vanden Daelen is a post doctoral researcher at the History Department, University of Antwerp, associated with the European Association for Jewish Studies. In 2008, her PhD-thesis on the the reconstruction of the Jewish Community in Antwerp after the Second World War (1944-1960), has been published by Aksant, Amsterdam ("Laten we hun lied verder zingen. De heropbouw van de Joodse gemeenschap in Antwerpen na de Tweede Wereldoorlog 1944-1960").

Wouter Veraart is professor of legal philosophy at the Department of Legal Theory and Legal History, VU University Amsterdam. In 2005, his PhD-thesis on the "Deprivation and restitution of property rights during the years of occupation and post-war reconstruction in the Netherlands and in France" (in Dutch) has been published by Kluwer, Deventer. He is currently working on a research project "Time, Restitution and the Law", for which a Veni-grant has been awarded by the Netherlands Organisation for Scientific Research.

Laurens Winkel is professor of Legal History at Erasmus University Rotterdam.

Name Index

Aalders, Gerard 107
Adenauer, Konrad 83-85, 87-89, 92
Andrieu, Claire 2, 3
Aristotle 8
Belinfante, W.G. 111
Bergen-Moll, Anna 49
Bergh, Gert-Jan van den 78
Blaustein, Jakob 89
Bloch-Bauer, Ferdinand 44
Bregstein, Marcel Henri 113, 115
Broek, A.A. ten 110
Cassin, René 13, 21, 27, 28, 32, 33
Citroen, Michal 96, 105
Cowen, Tyler 10
Dehler, Thomas 85
Donner, J.P.H. 113, 115
Dubbink, C.W. 116
Dworkin, Ronald 120
Eberstaller, Marie 49, 51, 55, 57, 58, 60, 61, 71-73
Eberstaller, Richard 49, 51, 55, 57, 58
Eggens, Jannes 25, 114, 116, 117, 119, 120
Ehrenzweig, Adolf 52, 53, 75
Fürsinn, Werner 78
Gadamer, Hans-Georg 120
Gaulle, Charles de 12, 13, 24, 27, 32, 33
Gehrer, Elisabeth 63
Goldmann, Nahum 89
Göring, Hermann 110, 112
Goudstikker, Desi *see* Von Saher, Desi
Goudstikker, Jacques 6, 109-113, 119
Graf, Georg 4, 9, 67, 68
Grimschitz, Bruno 51, 56, 60, 73, 74
Gropius, Manon 50
Gropius, Walter 49, 50
Haider, Jörg 40
Hauriou, Maurice 9
Hébraud, Pierre 9
Hein, Otto 52
Hijmans, I.H. 116
Hilberg, Raul 23
Hirsch, Martin 90

Hoffmann, Josef 50
Javits, Jakob Koppel 89
Kant, Immanuel 9
Khol, Andreas 47
Kirkpatrick, Ivone A. 84
Klimt, Gustav 44
Korthals Altes, E.J. 109, 110
Küster, Otto 83, 88
Legler, Wilhelm 53, 56, 61
Lieftinck, Piet 26, 27, 31-33, 109
Lillteicher, Jürgen 4
Lucy, William 8
Mahler, Gustav 49
Mahler, Marina 48, 49, 60, 63, 67, 70, 78
Mahler-Werfel, Alma 47-62, 70-78
Mayer, Monika 60, 71
McCloy, John J. 84, 85
Meijer, Max 110-112
Meissel, Franz-Stefan 4, 9
Miedl, Alois 110-112
Molengraaff, W.L.P.A. 117
Moll, Carl 49, 51, 55-61, 71- 74
Montesquieu, Ch.-L. de Secondat baron de La Brède et de 121
Munch, Edvard 50, 52, 56, 59
Oberhammer, Paul 78
Oppenheim, Paul 117
Pétain, Philippe 24
Pierlot, Hubert Marie Eugène 95
Radbruch, Gustav 113
Rawls, John 9
Roosevelt, Franklin Delano 27
Sanders, Heiman 21, 31-33
Schepper, Armand de 97
Schiele, Egon 40
Schindler, Jakob Emil 49, 50, 52, 55-57, 60
Schmid, Carlo 88
Schmied, Claudia 78
Scholten, Paulus 120
Schoordijk, H.C.F. 5, 6, 9, 119-121
Schwarz, Heinrich 50, 59, 61, 74
Seyss-Inquart, Arthur 22
Soeteman, Arend 6
Spier, E. 112
Steger, Alfred 79, 84, 86, 88, 90

Name Index

Sterngold, Jozef 97
Sternheim, A. 110
Suyling, J.P. 116
Terroine, Émile 21, 30-32
Vanden Daelen, Veerle. 5
Von Saher, Desi 6, 110, 112, 113
Veegens, D.J. 109, 112
Veraart, Wouter 4, 101, 116, 117, 119-121
Wagner-Gebauer, Ida 53
Waldron, Jeremy 10
Weinrib, E.J. 8
Werfel, Franz 49-51, 57
Wiederin, Ewald 78
Wilhelmina, Queen of the Netherlands 24, 27
Wittgenstein, Ludwig 120

Subject Index

Adenauer Government 87, 89
Administration des Domaines, see State Property Department
AJC *see* American Jewish Committee
Allgemeines VerwaltungsverfahrensG see General Administrative
    Procedure Act
Allied Control Council.. 83
Allied restitution programme.. 84, 91
American Jewish Committee (AJC) 89
American Military Government... 83
American State Departement 89
Annulment Act 1946 (Austria) *see* nullity acts
Anschluss... 50
anti-Semitism 89, 94
appeal and cassation.. 25, 30
Arbitral Authority for Restitution in Kind (Austria).................. 76
arbitration.. 25
arbitration panel 42-45
Archives of Vienna 48
Art Restitution Act 1998 (Austria) *see* restitution acts
Art Restitution Advisory Board (Austria).....48, 49, 60-64, 66, 68, 70, 77, 78
Aryanization..............................35, 36, 38, 40, 42, 44, 63, 80, 82, 87, 89-92
Aryanization tax.. 36
Association of Jews in Belgium... 93, 94
AusfuhrverbotsG see legislation, Export Ban Act
Austrian Gallery of the Belvedere in Vienna...... 47, 50-61, 67-71, 73, 75, 78
Austrian National Fund *see* National Fund of the Republic of Austria for
authority of decided cases *see* legally binding
AVG *see* legislation, General Administrative Procedure Act
'bad faith' owners 13, 15, 16, 29, 32
bank accounts.. 17, 101, 102
Bavarian Christian Social Union (CSU)................................... 85
Belvedere Museum Vienna *see* Austrian Gallery
    of the Belvedere in Vienna
Besluit Herstel Rechtsverkeer *see* restitution acts, Decree of 17 September
    1944 on the Restoration of Legal Relations
bewariërs see person of confidence
Bindungswirkung see legally binding
bona fide see good faith, purchases/acquisitions in
Breitenstein villa 51, 52, 73
British military authorities 83
BrüG-law *see BundesrückerstattungsG*

Brüsseler Treuhandgesellschaft (BTG) 101
Bundesgerichthof 84
BundesrückerstattungsG (BrüG-law) 104
Bundestag 84, 85, 87-92
Bundesverband für loyale Restitution 84
burden of proof 13, 29, 82
Bürgerliches Gesetzbuch see legislation, German Civil Code
businesses, spoliation of 35
Caisse des dépôts et consignations 18
Civil Code *see* legislation
CIVS, *see* French Commission for the Compensation of Victims of Spoliation
class actions 2, 17, 19, 40
Code of Civil Procedure (Austria) 67
Cold War 17
collection points 39
Commission of Provenance Research (Austria) 40, 60, 67, 70, 71, 75
Comittee on the Investigation of WW-II Assets 31
compensation for restitutors 12, 85-93
confiscation by the State 84
Conseil d'Etat 13, 16
Cottonwood Alley see paintings
Council of Restoration of Rights (NL) 26, 96, 99, 114
    Administration Division 26
    Immovable Property Division 26, 99
    Judicial Division 26, 27, 31, 32, 111
    Securities Division 26, 27
Cour Supérieure pour les restitutions 84
court decision *see* extremely unjust court decision
CSU *see* Bavarian Christian Social Union
death certificates 98, 99, 103, 106, 107
Decree E100 *see* restitution acts, Decree on the restoration of legal relations
Deutsche Bundestag see Bundestag
Dienst Economische Recuperatie *see* Economic Recuperation Service
Dienst van het Sekwester (Belgium) 102
duress 13, 29, 81, 82, 100
Dutch Central Bank 22, 26, 31
Dutch Stockbrokers' Association 22, 26, 27
economic reconstruction 11, 22, 26, 32, 34
Economic Recuperation Service 104
Eggens Committee 25, 26
EntschädigungsfondsG see General Settlement Fund Law
Entziehungsvermutung 82, *see also* duress

Subject Index

equality before the law, principle of 2, 3, 17, 32
equality of burdens, principle of 86, 91
equity 2, 6, 18, 19, 25, 117. 119-121
expropriation 23, 61, 64, 80
extreme injustice/ extremely unjust
    concept of 4, 6, 42, 43, 76, 77
    court decision 42, 43, 48, 60, 76
    settlement out-of-court 42-46, 76
fair price 29, 68, 81, 87, 90, 91
fast-track procedure 13, 15, 30
Federal Association for Loyal Restitution 79
Federal Court, German *see Bundesgerichthof*
Federal Democratic Party 79, 84, 85
Federal Ministry of Education and Culture in Austria 60, 63, 66
Federal Law Office (Austria) 52-54, 56, 57, 60, 61
Federal Restitution Law (West Germany) 88
Finanzprokuratur see Federal Law Office
forced sales *see* withdrawal of property
Forest Path see paintings
Forest Road in the Salzkammergut see paintings
Forest Road near St. Gilgen see paintings
Freedom Party (Austria) 40
Free France 12, 13, 27
French Commission for the Compensation of Victims of Spoliation
    (CIVS) 18
French Committee for National Liberation 13
French National Committee 24, 28, 33
From Corfu see paintings
Gallery of the 19th Century *see* Austrian Gallery of the
    Belvedere in Vienna
General Commission of Jewish Affairs (Vichy) 23
German parliament *see Deutsche Bundestag*
German State 15, 33, 36
good faith, purchases/acquisitions in 15, 16, 30, 32, 39, 58, 60, 65,
    66, 68, 69, 71-74, 81, 82, 85, 88, 96, 99, 100, 103, 117, 119
Government-in-exile:
    Belgian 95
    Dutch 24, 33, 96
Hacking Meadow see paintings
heirless property 63, 82, 83
Historical Commission (Austria) 40, 41
Historikerkommission see Historical Commission
hongerwinter 34
household effects 41, 93, 103, 104

housing restitution..95-99, 111
ICHEIC *see* International Commission on Holocaust-Era
    Insurance Claims
I.G. Farben 90
immovable property *see* housing restitution
independency of the courts 32
inequality of bargaining power 43
inequality of treatment 18, 19, 64
injustice *see* extreme injustice
Inter-Allied Agreement, 1946 Paris.. 15
Inter-Allied Declaration of 5 January 1943 .... 12, 24, 25, 28
intergovernmental agreement between France and the
    United States of 12 January 2001 19
intermediary agents *see* persons of confidence
International Commission on Holocaust-Era Insurance Claims
    (ICHEIC)...17, 18
Überleitungsvertrag... 88
Jewish (restitution) successor organizations.. 82, 83
Jews:
    assimilation, degree of... 107, 108
    'enemy' refugees.. 15
    nationality 15, 107, 108
    persecution 90, 93
    survival rate... 23
    victim organizations 29
Joint Declaration of St James *see* Inter-Allied Declaration
    of 5 January 1943
Judenvermögensabgabe.. 36, 87
justice:
    concept of... 43
    corrective 2-4, 15, 17, 19
    distributive 3, 4, 7, 8, 15, 17-19
*Kommission zur Erforschung der Provenienzen in den Österreichischen
    Bundesmuseen see* Commission of Provenance Research in Austrian
    Federal Museums
Kunstrückgabebeirat see Art Restitution Advisory Board
KunstrückgabeG see restitution acts, Austrian Art Restitution Act 1998
Lastenausgleich see common equality of burdens
Law on Damages caused by Reparations, Restitution, Destruction and
    Internal Restitution *see* Reparationsschädengesetz
legality, re-establishing of (France) 21, 22, 28, 29, 32
legally binding 9, 62, 67, 70, 76
legislation:
    Austrian General Administrative Procedure Act 63

Austrian General Civil Code 55, 65, 69, 71, 72, 77
Dutch Civil Code 22, 110, 111
Dutch Code of Civil Procedure 10
Export Ban Act 1918 (Austria) 62
French budgetary law 1948 15
French Civil Code 22
French Decree on the re-establishment of the republican legality
    of 9 August 1944 .... 13, 28, 29
French war damages law 1946 15
German Civil Code 81
inheritance laws, German 82
Nuremberg Laws 81
ReparationsschädenG (RepG) 90, 91
see also nullity acts
see also restitution acts
see also spoliation acts
levies, discriminatory 81, 87
life insurance policies 17, 31
limitation, statute of 17
Lippmann, Rosenthal & Co., Sarphatistraat *see* Liro bank
Liro bank 22, 23, 27, 30, 31, 102, 104
looting institutions (in the Netherlands) 30, 31
Mattéoli commission *see* Study Mission on the spoliation
    of Jews in France
Minister of Culture and Education, Austria 78
Minister of Finance, Netherlands 26, 27, 31-33, 109
Ministry of Finance, Belgium 102
Ministry of Finance, West-Germany 86
Möbelaktion 95, 101, 102, 105
Moonrise in the Prater see paintings
movable property 41, 58, 68, 69, 71, 72, 94, 95, 101-106
National Council of the Resistance 16
National Fund of the Republic of Austria for
    Victims of National Socialism 41, 47, 63
National Trust Fund (NL) 109, 111, 112, 114, 117
*Nationalfonds der Republik Österreich für Opfer des
    Nationalsozialismus see* National Fund of the Republic
        of Austria for Victims of National Socialism
NBI *see* National Trust Fund
Nederlands Beheersinstituut (NBI) *see* National Trust Fund
Netherlands Institute for War Documentation (NIOD) 109
NichtigkeitsG see nullity acts, Austrian Annulment Act 1946
NIOD *see* Netherlands Institute for War Documentation
nullity:

of extremely unjust decisions 62
  of legal transactions 9, 13, 28, 64, 66
nullity acts:
  Austrian Annulment Act 1946 .... 37, 52, 62, 63-68, 70
  Belgian Decree of 10 January 1941 95
  Dutch Decree of 7 June 1940 (Decree A6) 96, 111-114
  Dutch Decree of 17 September 1944 (Decree E93) 25
  French Decree on the re-establishment of the republican
      legality of 9 August 1944.. 13, 28
  French nullity acts... 13
Nuremberg Laws.. 81
Oberste Rückstellungskommission see Restitution Commissions
  in Austria, Supreme Restitution Commission
Ordonnance du 9 août 1944, see nullity acts, French Decree
  on the re-establishment of the republican legality
Ordonnance du 21 avril 1945, see restitution acts, French
  restitution decree of 21 April 1945
Österreichische Historikerkommission, see Historical Commission
paintings:
  Cottonwood Alley.. 56, 59
  Forest Path.. 50
  Forest Road in the Salzkammergut 56
  Forest Road near St. Gilgen 50
  From Corfu 56
  Hacking Meadow 56
  Moonrise in the Prater... 56
  Rocky coast near Ragusa... 50, 52, 54, 59
  Summer Night on the Beach by Edvard Munch 47-51, 55-62, 64,
                                                                                                      66-73, 75-78
passage of time 2-10, 92
persecution as collective offense 85, 86
persons of confidence 72, 73, 105, 106
Pierre, Arthur, Antwerp removal firm 103, 104
political persecution by the National Socialists 66, 74
prescription 2, 7-10
private autonomy in contract law 45
private ownership of property 12
Provenance Research Commission see Commission of Provenance
  Research in Austrian Federal Museums
Provisional Advisory Assembly (France).. 28, 29, 33
purchase price
  free access to 81, 87, 90
  see also fair price
Raad voor het Rechtsherstel see Council of Restoration of Rights

reasonableness..25, 119-121
référé see fast-track procedure
Reichsfluchtsteuer 36, 87
Reparationsschädengesetz (RepG) 90, 91
res iudicata see legally binding
responsibility of successor state.. 86
restitution:
    exceptionality..30
    normality..30
    process.. 11, 22, 32, 34, 103, 107
    results 11, 31, 107
    settlements...76
    time limit...12
restitution acts:
    Allied restitution laws 79, 80, 84, 85, 88, 89
    Austrian Art Restitution Act 1998 .... 40, 47, 48, 60, 61, 64, 65,
        67, 68, 70, 71, 77, 78
    Austrian General Settlement Fund Law 2001 .... 41, 43, 47, 48, 60, 76, 77
    Austrian National Fund Law 1995..47
    Austrian Reconciliation Fund Act 2000 40
    Austrian restitution acts 37-39, 41, 52
    Austrian Third Restitution Act 1947 .... 37, 52, 55, 58, 61,
        65-69, 71, 72, 74, 75
    Belgian restitution acts... 100
    BundesrückerstattungsG (BrüG-law) (West Germany)...................... 104
    Dutch Decree of 17 September 1944 on the Restoration
        of Legal Relations (Decree E100)...................... 26, 96, 103, 111, 116
    Dutch Decree of 16 November 1945 (Decree F272)................ 26, 96, 103
    Federal Restitution Law (West Germany) 88
    French restitution acts 13, 14, 16, 29
    French restitution decree of 21 April 1945 .... 13, 16, 29, 32
    preparation of Dutch restitution acts...25-27
    preparation of French restitution acts 27-30
Restitution Commission of Vienna..52-56, 61, 70
restitution courts
    in Austria *see* Restitution Commission of Vienna *and* Upper Restitution
        Commission
    in the Netherlands *see* Council of Restoration of Rights
RC Vienna *see* Restitution Commission of Vienna
Rocky Coast near Ragusa see paintings
ROK *see* Upper Restitution Commission of Vienna
Rückerstattungsgeschädigten..86
Rückstellungsoberkommission Wien *see* Upper Restitution
    Commission of Vienna

rule of law, re-establishing of 21, 22
safe deposit boxes 101
Sammelstellen see collection points
Scholten Commission *see* Comittee on the Investigation of
    WW-II Assets
securities 23, 27, 30, 31, 101, 102, 103, 107, 111
Service of Restitutions 30, 31
settlement, out-of-court...27, 42-46, 59, 112, 113
shares *see* securities
Shoah...17, 20
Social Democratic Party 88, 90
spoliation
    acts 101
    concept 23, 24
    process *see* Aryanization
    nullity *see* nullity, nullity acts
State ownership (France) 16
State Property Department.. 14
statutes of limitation...2, 18, 19
Stock Exchange:
    Amsterdam 22, 27, 31, 102
    Paris...30
Study Mission on the spoliation of Jews in France.......................................21, 23
successor state responsibility 86
Summer Night on the Beach see paintings
Supreme Court (Austria).. 77
Supreme Court of Administrative Law (Austria) 78
Supreme Restitution Commission (Austria) 38, 56, 75, 89
tenants:
    amicable arrangements 100
    compensation 41
    restitution 14, 100, 101
    tenancy agreements...38, 99
third parties, protection of..26, 119
time limit...12, 67
trauma
    war trauma 106, 107
    trauma of Versailles *see* Versailles
unequal treatment *see* inequality of treatment
United States:
    claims in..41
    class actions 40
    intervention 17
    negotiations 42

Upper Regional State Court (Austria) 57, 61
Upper Restitution Commission of Vienna (Austria) 48, 53-55, 58,
    61, 62, 70, 71-76
URC *see* Upper Restitution Commission of Vienna
Verband der Rückerstattungsgeschädigten 84
Vereeniging van Joden in België (VJB) *see* Association
    of Jews in Belgium
Vergangenheitspolitik 87, 92
Vermögensverkehrsstelle 36
Vermögensverwaltungs- und Rentenanstalt (VVRA) 23
Versailles, trauma of 83
VersöhnungsfondsG, see restitution acts, Austrian
    Reconciliation Fund Act 2000
Vichy 11, 22-24, 28, 29, 33
victim thesis 38
victims of restitution, self-proclaimed 84, 91
victors' justice 80, 83, 91
Volksgemeinschaft 80, 92
VVRA *see Vermögensverwaltungs- und Rentenanstalt*
Wiener Stadt- und Landesarchiv see Archives of Vienna
withdrawal of property 66-72, 95
World Jewish Congress (WJC) 89, 104

www.ingramcontent.com/pod-product-compliance
Ingram Content Group UK Ltd.
Pitfield, Milton Keynes, MK11 3LW, UK
UKHW051652180426
11947UKWH00021B/1917